D1566902

Create lasting memories!

Lynn Wilson

AT EASE

A Salute to Creative Entertaining

LYNN R. WILSON

Published by
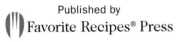 Favorite Recipes® Press
An imprint of
 SOUTHWESTERN Publishing Group®
P.O. Box 305142
Nashville, Tennessee 37230
1-800-358-0560

Food Photography: Stephen DeVries

Food Styling: Julia Rutland

Additional photography: Shutterstock (pages 37, 48, 65, 70, 77, 94, 97, 110, 123, 128, 130, 161, 177, 188, 195)

Cover and interior design, and page composition: pixiedesign, llc / Rikki Campbell Ogden

Editorial Director: Sheila Thomas

Recipe Editor: Nicki Pendleton Wood, CCP

Proofreader and Indexer: Linda Brock

Neither the United States Marine Corps nor any other component of the Department of Defense has approved, endorsed, or authorized this book.

ISBN: 978-0-87197-636-9

Library of Congress Control Number: 2015935224

Manufactured in the United States of America

First Printing: 2015

★ ACKNOWLEDGMENTS ★

This entertainment cookbook would not have been possible without the contributions and support of so many family and friends. The menus are compilations of recipes shared with me over the years by family and friends. Good food and drink has always been the cornerstone of our gatherings, and we love to share our favorite recipes with each other. I wish I had made a note of every person whose gift of a recipe was included here. If you recognize your recipe as you go through *At Ease*, know that I am deeply grateful for it.

My sister, Lucy Rockwood Smith, was instrumental in turning twenty-plus years of book talk into this real book you hold in your hands. She has listened to me talk for two decades, and she took the lead in convincing me to sit down and do it. Lucy is known for her creative parties and her wonderful cooking, so together we brainstormed party ideas and menus. Lucy and I watched our mother entertain through the years and have since had countless parties together. It is a special bond that the two of us have and I cherish it!

My husband, Bob, and our children, Elizabeth Wilson Chappell and Brian Wilson, have been so patient through this whole process of writing *At Ease*. They too encouraged me to follow my dream of writing it. Bob and I spent thirty-eight wonderful years in the Army. Finding creative ways to entertain was our way of making our assignments fun and our units close-knit. We have continued our fun and creative entertaining in civilian life and have made wonderful friends. Nothing brings people together better than a good party!

Thank you to my "Taste Bud" friends for your inspiration and enthusiasm, and for diligently testing and retesting so many recipes.

Lastly, when I began this journey, I had no idea what the book process involved. My wonderful publisher, Sheila Thomas, has guided me every step of the way with such patience and professionalism. The beautiful pictures in *At Ease* were a team effort of Photographer Stephen DeVries and his assistant Jake Blount, along with Food Stylist Julia Rutland and her assistant Callie Aldridge. Their team spent three crazy, wonderful days at our home in Alabama preparing, styling, and shooting the beautiful photographs for me. They are definitely the "A Team"! And thank you to the editorial and art team who turned my collection of recipes and ideas into a book: Nicki Wood for editing, Linda Brock for proofreading, and Rikki Campbell Ogden for the amazing job she did designing this book. Thank you for going above and beyond for this project and for being a delight to work with.

LEFT TO RIGHT | Stephen DeVries, Lucy and Wayne Smith, Callie Aldridge, Lynn and Bob Wilson, Sheila Thomas, Julia Rutland, Jake Blount

My ongoing gratitude goes to those who serve our country and to their families. Not many Americans realize that less than 1 percent of our population volunteers to serve in the military. We often forget that their families serve alongside them with their support and sacrifices. We all owe them a huge debt of gratitude! It is that family dynamic that was my inspiration to write At Ease!

★ CONTENTS ★

Happy Birthday

TO ALL OUR COUNTRY'S MILITARY SERVICES
ESTABLISHED ON THE FOLLOWING DATES:

 **ARMY** | JUNE 14, 1775

 **COAST GUARD** | AUGUST 4, 1790

 **MARINES** | NOVEMBER 10, 1775

 **NAVY** | OCTOBER 13, 1775

 **AIR FORCE** | SEPTEMBER 18, 1947

Introduction

Military life has so many challenges with the constant moves, deployments, and family separations; that is why I think entertaining is so important! It brings people together in a relaxing atmosphere where they can have fun! A lot has changed in the military over the thirty-eight years we were traveling from installation to installation, but one thing that has stayed constant is the need to be with friends and have fun. It is my hope that *At Ease* will be your guide for doing just that.

My biggest compliment is to run into old Army friends and have them tell me what a wonderful time they had when we were together and how they remember this party or that party. It makes me smile!

Although *At Ease* is written with the military in mind, it is a great entertainment cookbook for anyone who enjoys entertaining, as well as those wanting to learn. I have done many of these parties with our civilian friends since Bob retired, and all of the parties translate well into civilian life. Our friends love them! "Secret Valentine" has been one of their favorites! We also started the "Wheelbarrow Brigade," and it has been a fantastic success in our neighborhood. It has been ongoing for more than three years.

A portion of the sale from each cookbook will be donated to the installation where the cookbook is sold, to be used for their military family programs. It is my way of giving back and saying "thank you" to those who are still serving.

I hope you enjoy *At Ease: A Salute to Creative Entertaining* as much as I enjoyed writing it.

This original oil painting by Pat Matthews was a retirement gift presented to Bob by our children. The painting depicts Bob's Army career. On the left-hand side of the painting is a Purple Heart, which Bob earned in Vietnam. The cross sabers signify Cavalry, which were the units Bob commanded: 1/4 Cavalry and 3dACR. In the upper right of the painting is the Pentagon, Bob's last assignment in the Army. The three stars represent his retirement rank: Lieutenant General.

About the Author

I was born in Bloomington, Indiana. My father was in the Army, so I spent the first twelve years of my life as an "Army brat." I have a sister, Lucy, and two brothers, Rocky and Jeff. We all grew up watching our mom and dad entertain, so I came by my love of entertaining through them.

Lynn and Bob Wilson

Bob was in the Army for thirty-eight years. We were blessed with so many exciting tours. Bob was an Armor/Cavalry officer and we had tours in Germany, Hawaii, and Cairo, Egypt, and had various continental U.S. assignments. We loved every tour we had! Our children, Brian and Elizabeth, were both born when we were at Fort Hood, Texas. Until they were in college, they went with us to every installation. Elizabeth attended four different high schools, which is never easy, but she would "land" at our new posting and immediately be knocking on doors to meet new friends. Both of our children say they would not trade their military upbringing for anything. Brian decided to continue in the Army and went to West Point. Elizabeth was ready to settle down, so she went to the University of Texas. They both have married wonderful spouses who share their love of cooking and entertaining. Our six grandchildren, Jack, Sam, Ty, Adalynn, Austin, and Luke, have grown up cooking with me (Nana) and insisted that "Wilson Burgers" be included in the cookbook.

Lynn

"Lynn has shared a unique and special aspect of military life, that creates lifelong memories, connections, and friendships, by gathering neighbors, units, and even strangers into your home. Her creative party planning ideas and well-tested recipes in At Ease: A Salute to Creative Entertaining makes it easy and fun to ensure everyone feels welcomed, comfortable, and included—a great way to build teams and to support one another during good times and the tough ones!"

—PATTY SHINSEKI, Wife of former Chief of Staff of the Army, General Eric Shinseki

New Year's Day Brunch

New Year's Day receptions have always been a military tradition. It is a wonderful way to bring in the New Year and set the tone for the upcoming year. Instead of a stand-up cocktail affair, my husband and I had a New Year's Brunch one year that was such a hit that it became our yearly tradition.

Most of the recipes in the following menu can be prepared ahead of time and frozen, making it easier on the host. Pick and choose the ones best suited for your reception.

INVITATION

Invitations can be formal military-style invitations, or you can create your own with one of the many online templates available. For a splashy and different invitation, visit a local party store for plastic champagne glasses, fill them with glitzy confetti, and tuck the invitation inside. Delivering them personally takes a little more effort, but it gets guests excited about the upcoming event.

For a short guest list, a single arrival time is customary. For a big crowd, consider staggered arrival times so that you have smaller groups. You want to be able to visit with each guest and offer a New Year's greeting. The traditional receiving line is always an option if you are having a large group; however, if you decide to go with smaller groups, I would forgo the receiving line and make sure you get around to each of your guests.

DECORATIONS

Decorating with a combination of military unit items and New Year's decorations is always fun. My husband commanded cavalry units, so I tucked red and white guidons, unit flags, Stetsons, and spurs among starbursts of the New Year. Simple stand-up frames around the room showcased unit events from the past year.

ACTIVITY

A New Year military gathering is a time to thank guests for the past year and to look forward to the New Year. To add an activity, it's fun for guests to fill out New Year's resolutions capsules. For each guest, have a short cardboard tube (such as a toilet paper roll) wrapped in decorative paper with one end closed and tied with ribbon. Guests write resolutions on slips of paper. They can be personal or related to the unit—either way, no one else will see them. The resolutions go into the "capsules," which are then tied shut with ribbon. Provide labels so guests can identify their capsules. Collect the capsules and pass them out at the following New Year's reception or when a couple leaves the unit.

★ MENU ★

Moose Milk

A favorite at our holiday receptions since the 1970s.

2½ cups brandy

1¼ cups dark rum

1¼ cups light rum

1¼ cups crème de cacao

3 quarts eggnog

2 quarts whole milk

1 pint vanilla ice cream

Ground nutmeg

Combine the brandy, dark rum, light rum and crème de cacao in a resealable plastic bag the day before the party so the flavors meld. Right before the party begins, pour the liquor into the punch bowl. Add the eggnog and milk and stir. Add the ice cream and stir gently. To serve, ladle some Moose Milk into a punch cup and sprinkle with nutmeg.

YIELD | 35 (6-ounce) cups

• • •

Bloody Mary Punch

An easy way to serve Bloody Marys.

8 cups vegetable juice or tomato juice

1 cup vodka

⅓ cup Worcestershire sauce

½ cup fresh lemon juice (about 4 lemons)

½ cup fresh lime juice (about 5 limes)

2 tablespoons celery seed

Hot red pepper sauce to taste

GARNISH

Lemon and lime wheels

½ teaspoon freshly ground black pepper

Combine the vegetable juice, vodka, Worcestershire sauce, lemon juice, lime juice, celery seed and pepper sauce in a punch bowl. Cover and chill for at least 3 hours before serving. Float lemon and lime wheels in the punch. To serve, ladle some of the punch into a punch cup and sprinkle with a pinch of the pepper.

YIELD | 10 (8-ounce) servings

• • •

Percolator Punch

Perfect alcohol-free punch for a large group.

32 ounces cranberry juice

46 ounces pineapple juice

46 ounces apple juice

2 cups water

1 lemon, sliced

3 cinnamon sticks

2 tablespoons whole cloves

¾ cup brown sugar

Combine the cranberry juice, pineapple juice, apple juice and water in the bottom of a large electric percolator. Place the lemon, cinnamon sticks, cloves and brown sugar in the percolator basket. Turn on the percolator. When it completes the cycle, the punch is hot and ready to serve.

YIELD | 16 (1-cup) servings

Cavalry Champagne Punch

This recipe was labeled "Top Secret" when it was given to me.

½ liter vodka, chilled

2 liters ginger ale, chilled

1 (750-ml) bottle Chablis, chilled

4 (750-ml) bottles champagne, chilled

GARNISH

Orange and lemon wheels

2 cups fresh raspberries

Combine the vodka, ginger ale and Chablis in a punch bowl. Add the champagne just before serving (or as guests arrive). Float orange and lemon wheels in the punch. To serve, place fresh raspberries in each glass or punch cup and top with punch.

YIELD | 35 (6-ounce) cups

• • •

Coffee with a Chocolate Cloud

A dollop of Chocolate Cloud atop a hot cup of coffee is so yummy!

4 ounces German's sweet chocolate

1 (14-ounce) can sweetened condensed milk

8 ounces heavy whipping cream

Freshly brewed coffee

Heat the chocolate with the condensed milk in a small saucepan over low heat, until the chocolate melts, stirring constantly. Let the mixture cool. Whip the cream to stiff peaks. Gently fold in the cooled chocolate mixture. Spoon the mixture into a serving bowl and place next to a pot of coffee. Guests place a dollop of Chocolate Cloud on top of a steaming cup of coffee.

YIELD | enough to top 36 cups of coffee

• • •

Mini Cinnamon Rolls

Easy and delicious!

1 (8-ounce) package crescent roll dough

1 teaspoon cinnamon

2 tablespoons brown sugar

½ cup (1 stick) margarine or butter, softened

¼ cup finely chopped nuts (optional)

Preheat the oven to 350 degrees. Separate the crescent rolls into 4 rectangles, pressing the perforations to seal. Combine the cinnamon and brown sugar. Spread 2 tablespoons of the butter over each rectangle. Sprinkle the cinnamon sugar over the butter. Add nuts, if desired. Roll up each rectangle, starting at the long side. Cut each roll into 5 slices and place cut side up in lightly greased mini muffin cups. Bake for 15 to 17 minutes.

YIELD | 20 mini rolls

EGG SAUCE ON CORN BREAD

Egg Sauce on Corn Bread

An unusual brunch entrée.

CORN BREAD

1¼ cups all-purpose flour

¾ cup cornmeal

¼ cup sugar

2 teaspoons baking powder

½ teaspoon salt

1 cup skim milk, whole milk or buttermilk

¼ cup vegetable oil

1 egg, beaten

EGG SAUCE

3 tablespoons butter

3 tablespoons flour

1 cup milk

1 cup half-and-half

⅛ teaspoon pepper

6 hard-boiled eggs, chopped

½ cup mayonnaise

GARNISH

Chopped green onions, crumbled bacon, chopped tomatoes, grated cheese, picante sauce or salsa and chopped avocado

For the corn bread, preheat the oven to 400 degrees. Grease a 9-inch baking pan. Combine the flour, cornmeal, sugar, baking powder and salt in a bowl and mix well. Stir in the milk, oil and egg and mix until dry ingredients are moistened. Pour the batter into the prepared pan. Bake for 20 to 25 minutes or until lightly golden brown and wooden pick inserted in the center comes out clean.

For the Egg Sauce, melt the butter in a large pan over low heat. Add flour, stirring until smooth. Cook for 1 minute, stirring constantly. Gradually add the milk and half-and-half. Cook until thickened and bubbly, stirring constantly. Add the pepper, eggs and mayonnaise. Heat thoroughly without boiling.

To serve, cut the corn bread into squares or wedges and slice each serving horizontally into halves. Let guests serve themselves corn bread, topping it with the egg mixture and desired garnishes.

YIELD | 9 servings

Note
The Egg Sauce recipe doubles well.

STRONGER SHELLS | To prevent egg shells from cracking when hard-boiling eggs, add a pinch of salt to the water.

Mini Broccoli Quiches

These may be made ahead of time and frozen.

Pastry for 2 (9-inch) pies

2 tablespoons butter or margarine, melted

1 (10-ounce) package frozen chopped broccoli, thawed

½ cup shredded Swiss cheese

1 cup half-and-half

3 eggs

1 teaspoon salt

Grease and flour 36 mini muffin cups. On a floured surface, roll the pastry with a rolling pin to about ⅛ inch thick. Use a fluted 3-inch round cookie cutter to make 36 circles, rerolling the pastry scraps. Place the pastry rounds in the muffin cups. Brush lightly with the butter. Refrigerate for 30 minutes or until thoroughly chilled.

Preheat the oven to 400 degrees. Drain the broccoli well on paper towels. Combine the broccoli and cheese in a bowl and mix well. Spoon about 1 teaspoon of the mixture into each muffin cup.

Whisk the half-and-half, eggs and salt in a medium bowl until well blended. Spoon about 1 tablespoon of the egg mixture into each muffin cup. Bake for 25 minutes or until a knife inserted in the center of a quiche comes out clean. Cool on a wire rack for about 15 minutes. Serve warm, or wrap and freeze.

YIELD | 36 quiches

Note

To reheat frozen quiches, preheat oven to 400 degrees. Unwrap and bake frozen quiches for 20 to 25 minutes or until heated through.

Tomato Bacon Cups

These little bites also make a terrific appetizer, and they freeze beautifully.

Nonstick cooking spray

1 pound bacon, chopped

½ onion, finely chopped

½ cup mayonnaise (do not use low fat)

1 medium tomato, peeled, seeded and chopped

5 ounces shredded Swiss cheese

1 (10-count) can Pillsbury Flaky biscuits, or Homemade Biscuit Dough (recipe follows)

Preheat the oven to 375 degrees. Spray mini muffin cups with cooking spray.

Cook the bacon in a medium skillet until crisp. Drain all but 1 tablespoon of the drippings from the skillet. Sauté the onion in the drippings until soft.

Combine the bacon, onion, mayonnaise, tomato and Swiss cheese in a small bowl and mix well.

Separate each biscuit into 3 thinner biscuits. Press each piece gently over the bottom and sides of a mini muffin cup. Fill the cups with bacon mixture. Bake for 10 to 12 minutes or until nicely browned. Serve warm, or wrap and freeze.

To use Homemade Biscuit Dough, spray mini muffin cups with nonstick cooking spray. Pinch off a small ball of dough and press over the bottom and up the side of each muffin cup. Fill with bacon mixture and cook according to the directions above.

YIELD | 30 cups

Note

To reheat frozen cups, place on a cookie sheet and bake at 375 degrees for 15 to 20 minutes or until heated through.

HOMEMADE BISCUIT DOUGH

½ cup (1 stick) butter, softened

3 ounces cream cheese, softened

1 cup all-purpose flour

Combine the butter and cream cheese in a bowl and mix well. Add the flour and mix to form a soft dough. Do not overmix. Wrap in plastic wrap and chill for 1 to 12 hours. Proceed with recipe.

Pineapple Cream Cheese Roll-Ups

Can be made ahead and frozen.

8 ounces cream cheese, softened

1 egg yolk, beaten

2 tablespoons sugar

1 teaspoon vanilla extract

1 (10-ounce) can crushed pineapple, drained and patted dry

14 or 15 pieces thin white bread, crusts trimmed

½ cup (1 stick) butter or margarine, melted

2 tablespoons cinnamon mixed with 1 cup sugar

Preheat oven to 350 degrees. Beat the cream cheese and egg yolk with an electric mixer until creamy. Add the sugar, vanilla and pineapple and mix well.

Roll the bread slices flat with a rolling pin. Spread 1 tablespoon of the pineapple mixture on each bread slice. Roll jelly-roll style to enclose the filling. Cut into halves or thirds.

Dip the roll-ups in the butter and then roll in the cinnamon-sugar. (The roll-ups can be prepared to this point and frozen.)

To cook, place seam side down on a lightly greased baking sheet and bake for 10 to 12 minutes.

To cook from frozen, thaw and let come to room temperature before baking.

YIELD | 28 large roll-ups or 45 small roll-ups

Easy Pecan Rolls

Gooey and delicious!

- 5 tablespoons butter or margarine, melted
- ¾ cup brown sugar
- ½ cup finely chopped pecans
- ¼ cup water
- 3 tablespoons butter or margarine, softened
- 2 (8-ounce) cans crescent roll dough
- ¼ cup sugar
- 2 teaspoons cinnamon

Preheat the oven 375 degrees. Spread the melted butter over the bottom of 9 × 13-inch baking pan. Sprinkle with the brown sugar, pecans and water. Set aside.

Separate each can of dough into 4 rectangles, pressing the perforations to seal. Spread the softened butter over the rectangles. Combine the sugar and cinnamon and sprinkle over the dough. Roll up each rectangle. Cut each into four pieces. Place cut side down in the prepared pan.

Bake for 20 to 25 minutes or until golden brown. Invert immediately onto a serving platter. Serve while still warm.

YIELD | 32 rolls

Fruit Kabobs
with Grand Marnier Sauce

A grown-up fruit salad.

FRUIT KABOBS

Assorted fresh fruit: strawberries, bananas, grapes, pineapple or whatever fresh fruit looks good, cut into bite-size chunks

6-inch wooden skewers

GRAND MARNIER SAUCE

- 8 ounces cream cheese
- 1 cup sour cream
- ¾ cup confectioners' sugar
- ½ cup heavy whipping cream
- 2 tablespoons Grand Marnier or more to taste

For the Fruit Kabobs, thread the fruit onto the skewers, alternating varieties.

For the Grand Marnier Sauce, combine the cream cheese, sour cream, confectioners' sugar, whipping cream and Grand Marnier in a food processor and process until blended and smooth, adding more Grand Marnier, if needed. Refrigerate until ready to use.

For a pretty presentation, arrange the Fruit Kabobs on a platter around a bowl of the Grand Marnier Sauce.

YIELD | 2 cups sauce

New Year, New You

The holidays are over, and it is now time to look forward to the brand new year ahead. What do you want to do? Lose weight? Get organized? Give back to your community? Let this year be the start of new beginnings. What better way to get committed than to do it with a group of friends and/or your unit? Host a New Year, New You luncheon, and brainstorm together what you would like to accomplish this year.

When we were stationed at Fort Knox, Kentucky, I worked with the installation to get a running track installed at the middle school. The school was located in an area without a good place for walking or running. As the middle school PE teacher, I wanted my students to be able to get outside and exercise.

Look around your installation or community. What is needed? Where could you, as a group, make a difference? My sister told me of a community that built a handicap-accessible playground so children with special needs would have a safe place to play. Is that something your community could benefit from?

How about partnering with your local school to plant a community garden? Growing vegetables is a great way to get children to eat healthier food. I have learned from gardening with my young grandchildren that if children are a part of planning and planting, they will eat the food!

★ MENU ★

"Pizza wheel" garden illustration by my brother, Clyde Jefferson Rockwood

A "pizza wheel" garden is one idea. A circular garden patch is divided into "slices," each planted with a vegetable or herb used in making pizza: onions, tomatoes, peppers, and herbs (like basil). Let the students decide what they want to grow and then have a pizza party after the harvest.

Another idea is to grow food to donate to a local food pantry. What a great experience for school children to learn to work and give back to their community.

There are endless project ideas; what's important is to pledge to make a difference in your community this year.

What about you as an individual? Commit to yourself as well. Try new things. Are you in an "eating rut," where you eat the same things all the time and maybe you aren't eating as healthfully as you would like? Try new foods. I have a menu for this month that gives you the opportunity to try new foods.

Another idea is to make "Promise Cards." Write out twelve cards, one for each month of the year. On each card write the phrase, "This month, I will...." Write things down things that you have put off that you really would like to do: take a Spanish course,

learn to salsa dance, go to a symphony or teach your children how to cook a family meal. Each month, pull a card out and work on it during the month. Have fun with it and use the cards to try new things.

INVITATION

Send out invitations asking your guests to be thinking about what they want to accomplish this year. Include a Promise Card and ask them to bring it with them to the luncheon.

DECORATIONS

Set up a table with your Promise Card boxes or bottles (or both). Include decorating materials, such as bright beads, trim and sequins.

ACTIVITY

Before your luncheon, take time to search out some of the needs of your installation and/or community. Pick up brochures and speak to the people running the organizations. Find out what they need and how your group can help. This information can get your discussion going at the luncheon.

Appoint someone at the luncheon to write down all the group's ideas. Discuss them to decide which ones your group would like to pursue. Try to narrow the focus to two or three ideas. Ask for volunteers to research each idea and bring the information to the next get-together. Build a timeline. When you have the necessary information, take a group vote on which project to undertake. I guarantee that your commitment to a community project will fulfill you in countless ways and make your New Year brighter!

Provide small jars or boxes to be decorated for the "Promise Cards." Give each person twelve "This month, I promise to _____" slips of paper for their promise cards.

Whiskey Cranberry Slushes

3 cups cranberry juice

2 cups whiskey, preferably Crown Royal

4½ cups pomegranate juice

2 cups orange juice

¼ cup lime juice

1 cup sugar

½ cup water

3 cups cranberry juice

1 cup fresh cranberries, diced

GARNISH

Mint leaves

Combine 3 cups cranberry juice, whiskey, pomegranate juice, orange juice, lime juice, sugar and water in a large shallow freezer-safe container and mix well. Cover and freeze for 4 to 5 hours or until the mixture is icy, stirring every 20 to 30 minutes.

Scrape the frozen mixture with a spoon and divide among glasses, filling them ¾ full. Divide 3 cups cranberry juice among the glasses and add diced cranberries; stir until slushy. Garnish with mint leaves.

YIELD | 10 to 12 drinks

Tortellini Caprese Bites

1 (9-ounce) package cheese tortellini

3 cups small grape tomatoes, cut into halves if large

3 (8-ounce) packages bocconcini

60 fresh basil leaves

60 (6-inch) wooden skewers

Basil Vinaigrette (recipe follows)

Prepare the tortellini according to the package directions. Drain and rinse under cold water.

Thread 1 tortellini, 1 tomato, 1 bocconcini and 1 basil leaf onto each skewer, arranging the skewers in a 9 × 13-inch dish. Pour the Basil Vinaigrette over the skewers to coat. Cover and chill for 2 hours.

Arrange the skewers on a platter, discarding any remaining vinaigrette.

YIELD | 60 bites

BASIL VINAIGRETTE

½ cup white balsamic vinegar

⅔ cup extra-virgin olive oil

6 tablespoons chopped fresh basil

Pour the vinegar into a small bowl. Add the olive oil in a slow steady stream, whisking until smooth. Stir in the basil.

Yield: 1½ cups

Tomato Soup
with Grilled Cheese Croutons

½ cup finely chopped leeks

1 rib of celery

2 garlic cloves, crushed

3 tablespoons butter

3 tablespoons all-purpose flour

3 cups chicken broth

1 (28-ounce) can Italian-style tomatoes

3 tablespoons tomato paste

6 fresh basil leaves

1 tablespoon minced fresh parsley

1 tablespoon sugar

1 bay leaf

Grilled Cheese Croutons (recipe follows)

Cook the leeks, celery and garlic in the butter in a Dutch oven until tender, stirring frequently. Reduce the heat to low and add the flour. Cook for 1 to 2 minutes, stirring constantly. Increase the heat to medium. Add the chicken broth gradually and cook until thickened, stirring constantly.

Chop the undrained tomatoes. Add the tomatoes, tomato paste, basil, parsley, sugar and bay leaf to the broth. Bring to a boil. Reduce the heat. Simmer, covered, for 45 minutes. Remove the bay leaf.

Process the soup in small batches in a food processor or blender until all of the soup is blended. Top servings with Grilled Cheese Croutons.

YIELD | 6 to 8 servings

GRILLED CHEESE CROUTONS

Butter

Pumpernickel bread

Thick-sliced sharp Cheddar cheese

Butter one side of a slice of pumpernickel bread. Place a slice of cheese on the unbuttered side. Top the cheese with another buttered slice of pumpernickel bread. Grill in a skillet until the cheese is melted and the bread is crispy and brown, turning once. Let stand to cool completely. Cut the sandwich into croutons using a mini cookie cutter or cut into small squares using a knife.

FIESTA CHICKEN SALAD

Fiesta Chicken Salad

FIESTA SEASONING

2½ teaspoons chili powder

1 tablespoon taco seasoning mix

½ teaspoon seasoned salt

1 teaspoon chipotle pepper

½ teaspoon cumin

SALAD

3 cups chopped tomato

¾ cup diced yellow bell pepper

¼ cup finely chopped red onion

1 tablespoon sugar

3 tablespoons cider vinegar

¼ teaspoon salt

⅛ teaspoon pepper

¼ cup lemon juice

¼ cup Dijon mustard

3 tablespoons water

1 tablespoon honey

4 (4-ounce) boneless skinless chicken
   breast halves

Nonstick cooking spray

16 ounces sugar snap peas, trimmed

8 cups torn romaine lettuce

For the Fiesta Seasoning, mix the chili powder, taco seasoning mix, seasoned salt, chipotle pepper and cumin in a small bowl.

For the Fiesta Chicken Salad, combine the tomato, bell pepper, onion, sugar, vinegar, salt and pepper in a bowl and toss to mix. Cover and chill.

Combine the lemon juice, Dijon mustard, water and honey in a large bowl and whisk to blend thoroughly. Cover and chill.

Rub the chicken with the Fiesta Seasoning. Coat a large heavy skillet with cooking spray and place over medium-high heat until hot. Add the chicken and cook for 7 minutes on each side or until the chicken is cooked through. (You may also grill the chicken on an outdoor grill.) Let stand to cool. Cut the chicken across the grain into thin slices.

Place the peas in a steamer basket over boiling water. Cover and steam for 2 minutes. Rinse under cold water; drain. Add the peas and lettuce to the lemon juice mixture and toss to coat. Divide the lettuce mixture among 4 large salad bowls. Top each with 1 cup tomato mixture and 1 sliced chicken breast half.

YIELD | 4 servings

Note

The Fiesta Seasoning may be stored in a resealable plastic bag.

TIPS

GREEN TO RED | To ripen green tomatoes, wrap them individually in a couple of sheets of newspaper. Store in an airtight container, in a dark place at room temperature. Check to see if ripened after 3 days.

Apple Muffins

This recipe came from my mother's friend. She always gave a muffin pan filled with this batter as a Christmas gift. The batter lasts well in the refrigerator for up to two weeks.

2 eggs, beaten

2 cups cubed fresh apples

½ cup vegetable oil

2 cups all-purpose flour

2 cups brown sugar

1½ teaspoons ground cinnamon

1½ teaspoons baking soda

1 teaspoon salt

Preheat the oven 350 degrees. Mix the eggs and apples in a large bowl. Stir in the oil.

Combine the flour, brown sugar, cinnamon, baking soda and salt in a bowl and mix well. Add to the apple mixture and mix well. Spoon into greased or paper-lined muffin cups, filling ¾ full.

Bake for 25 minutes or until a toothpick inserted into the center comes out clean.

YIELD | 24 muffins

TIPS

STRAWBERRY TRICK | To easily remove the green top from a strawberry, insert a plastic straw through the bottom of the strawberry up through the green section. The green top pops off smoothly, without removing any of the strawberry. (Kids will love to do this for you!)

Blackberry Cheesecake Parfaits

A light, delicious dessert!

1 cup light ricotta cheese

1 cup nonfat cream cheese

½ cup sugar

½ cup no-sugar-added all-fruit seedless blackberry spread

4 cups fresh blackberries

1½ cups vanilla wafer crumbs (about 40 cookies)

½ cup frozen reduced-calorie whipped topping, thawed

1 cup slivered almonds, toasted

Process the ricotta cheese, cream cheese and sugar in a food processor until smooth.

Heat the blackberry spread in a small saucepan until melted. Add the blackberries and stir gently.

Spoon ¼ cup of the blackberry mixture into each of eight 8-ounce parfait glasses. Layer each with 2 tablespoons ricotta mixture, 3 tablespoons wafer crumbs, ¼ cup blackberry mixture, 2 tablespoons ricotta mixture, and 1 tablespoon whipped topping. Chill parfaits for at least 2 hours. Sprinkle with toasted almonds before serving.

YIELD | 8 servings

Note

You may substitute whatever fruit and all-fruit spread you like. Fresh raspberries and raspberry spread make pretty parfaits, as do fresh strawberries and strawberry spread.

BLACKBERRY CHEESECAKE PARFAITS

Secret Valentine

Give yourself plenty of time to prepare for this Valentine surprise; the details are what make it so special.

I dreamed up Secret Valentine when my husband's unit was deployed to Iraq for Desert Shield/Desert Storm. It was the first war for most of the soldiers and their families, so it was a very stressful time. I wanted to do something special for both the soldiers and their spouses.

★ MENU ★

I sent each husband a questionnaire about his wife (how they met, quirks, etc.). I also made up individual Valentine Coupon Books—a very simple design with seven blank pages. I asked the husbands to write one thing they would do for their wife on each page. I also included a note card for each man to write a private Valentine note to his wife, and an envelope for both the coupon book and the note. I asked each man to write the note and put it and the coupon book in the envelope, seal it, and write his wife's name on the front of the envelope. (A sample questionnaire is included on page 25. It can be adapted easily for your group.)

I weighed the envelope, coupon book, note card, and questionnaire and included a postage-paid envelope for each man to mail the package back to me. I put everything in a 5 × 7 envelope with a letter explaining to the husbands what I planned and what I needed them to do. (A sample letter is included on page 24.) I emphasized that I needed the information by a certain date.

(Of course, I worried I might not get all of the envelopes back and some wives would be left out and heartbroken. However, I got every envelope back and all by the due date.)

Now, the fun part! I sent invitations to the wives asking them to join me for a Valentine party. I put together a heart-filled menu (page 20). The house was filled with Valentine decorations.

After the meal, I told the wives I had a special treat for them. I read a few questions and answers from the questionnaires and asked the group to guess who had answered the questions. The wives were flabbergasted to hear responses from their husbands. I handed each wife her envelope with a coupon book of seven items her husband promised to do after returning, the questionnaire with all the wonderful responses from her husband, and a private Valentine note. You can imagine the response—lots of happy tears!

Alternate Idea for "Secret Valentine"

Secret Valentine also works if husbands are not deployed—there's just a little twist to it. The challenge is getting the envelope to the husband without the wife seeing it. There are a couple of methods for doing this. One is to address the large envelope to the husband and add in big letters, "PRIVATE: FOR _____ ONLY!" so hopefully only the husband will open it. The other is to take the envelopes to the unit for them to distribute. The only hitch with this method is that it's only as reliable as the person you entrust with the distribution.

The questionnaires, coupon books, and envelopes are done the same as described above, but the party is a couple's party. The size of your group will determine whether you serve buffet foods or sit-down foods. This chapter includes plenty of both kinds of recipes.

A little extra preparation adds a sprinkling of fun to this evening. I had the questionnaires on my computer, and when the answers came back, I typed in the answers under the questions. The important thing here is to scramble the order of the answers so there is no pattern. For instance you don't want all of "Tom's" answers to be in the #4 spot. Wives will pick up on that very quickly. (I learned that the hard way one year.)

On the night of the party, I gave each wife a questionnaire with every husband's answers underneath and asked her to choose the answer she thought was her husband's. I tallied up the answers, and the couple with the highest score won a box of Valentine chocolates. The coupon books and notes were then handed out.

Whichever Secret Valentine party you host, the key to success is organization. Give yourself plenty of time to mail the envelopes so you can be sure to get them back by the due date. Set the due date for returned envelopes at least 2 weeks before the party so there's time to contact anyone who has not returned an envelope. You do not want anyone left out of this fun event!

Secret Valentine will be a memory maker for many of your guests. Couples still tell me years later how much it meant to them! Remember, the great thing about this party is that you can adjust it to fit your group. The questions on the questionnaire are just suggestions; change them to suit your group. Most of all, HAVE FUN!

INVITATION

Buy small boxes of chocolates (4 to 6 chocolates in a box), tuck the invitation inside, wrap the boxes in brown paper or tuck them into small mailing envelopes, and mail to your guests.

Want an inexpensive and cute invitation? Buy some fun printed Valentine paper (8½ × 11 inches); cut into 2 pieces (5½ × 8½ inches). Fold in half. On a separate piece of paper, cut out a 4 × 6-inch heart and print the invitation on the heart. Fold a 1 × 6-inch strip of paper accordion style. Tape or glue it inside the card and affix the heart to the other end of it. When the card opens up, the heart "pops" out. Place in an envelope, and mail to your guests.

DECORATIONS

Let red and white rule for this party! Cut out different size hearts in red and white. Cut fishing line to desired length. For example, if you want to hang hearts from a doorway for your guests to walk through, cut the line so it reaches from the top of the door to nearly the floor. Select a pair of matching hearts, then use double-sided tape to tape them, front and back, to the fishing line. Continue down the length of the line, varying the size and color of hearts you use. Tape the line to the top of the door.

Need a centerpiece? Go to your local craft store and buy LOVE wooden letters that will stand on their own. Paint them bright red, adding decorations, such as sequins, if desired. Use them on your table as a centerpiece. Or buy a heart form and glue "conversation hearts" all over the form. The ideas on Valentine's Day are endless!

Dear Husbands,

To make this an extra-special Valentine's Day, I would appreciate it if you would fill out this simple questionnaire. I am going to have some fun with it at the Valentine party. I am enclosing a stamped, self-addressed envelope for you to send back to me. I need the envelope back by _____(date) so that I have time to compile the results and put everything together before the party.

I have also enclosed a coupon book for you. All you have to do is fill out each page with something that you will do for your wife. For example: "I will cook you your favorite meal." or "I will give you a romantic massage." Whatever you would like to write. There are 7 coupons—one for each day of the week. I have also given you a note card so that you can write a Valentine note to your wife. Please put the coupon book and the note card in the white envelope I included. Seal it and write your wife's name on the front of the envelope. No one will see the coupon book or the note except for you and your wife. Put the small envelope and the questionnaire in the self-addressed, stamped envelope and mail it back to me.

Remember this is a secret for your wife. Please be sure that I receive the envelope by _____(date). Thank you!

QUESTIONNAIRE

1. I met my wife for the first time at:

2. When I saw her for the first time, I thought:

3. For our first date, we:

4. A perfect date with my wife would be:

    a) dinner and a movie

    b) dinner at home with a good rental movie, a bottle of wine, and a fire in the fireplace

    c) a romantic dinner at her favorite restaurant

    d) forget dinner and go straight to the bedroom with wine and a box of chocolates

    e) _____

5. What special "quirk" do you find endearing about your wife?

6. What would your wife say is your most endearing "quirk"? (No fair asking your wife for the answer!)

7. What is one thing you would like your wife to stop doing?

8. What one thing would your wife like you to stop doing?

9. The most attractive part of my wife is:

    a) eyes

    b) smile

    c) legs

    d) laugh

    e) body

    f) _____

10. If you had a free Saturday to spend with your wife, what would you plan from morning to night?

11. I would love for my wife to learn.....

12. If you were going to buy your wife a bouquet of flowers, what kind of flowers would she want?

13. What color do you think is most attractive on your wife?

14. What one word best describes your wife?

Your Name:

Wife's Name:

CURRIED SHRIMP CANAPÉS

Curried Shrimp Canapés

This is a great recipe to take to potluck. It always gets rave reviews!

1 baguette loaf, sliced ¼- to ½-inch thick
(most grocery stores will do this for you)

6 to 8 tablespoons olive oil

1 cup mayonnaise

¼ cup mango chutney, chopped

1 teaspoon curry powder

24 medium shrimp, cooked, peeled
and deveined

Cayenne pepper

Preheat the oven to 350 degrees.

Brush both sides of the bread with olive oil (or see Note). Bake the bread on the center oven rack for about 10 minutes until golden brown, turning after 5 minutes. Cool and cover until ready to use.

Combine the mayonnaise, chutney and curry powder in a small bowl and mix well. Chill until serving time.

Spread ½ tablespoon of chutney mixture on each bread slice. Cut a small slit up the middle of the shrimp to the tail. Fan the shrimp on top of the chutney mixture with the tail pointing up. Arrange on a serving platter and sprinkle lightly with cayenne pepper.

YIELD | 24 canapés

Note

To easily coat the bread with olive oil, spread the oil in an 11 × 14-inch baking pan. Arrange the bread in the pan and then turn the slices over to coat the other side.

CHAMPAGNE WITH HIBISCUS FLOWER

Place a hibiscus flower in each champagne glass. Fill with champagne and some hibiscus juice.

You can find hibiscus flowers in most liquor stores and specialty food stores.

Pumpkin Bisque

Warms you on those cold February days.

1 cup chopped onion

2 tablespoons butter

2 (14-ounce) cans chicken broth

3 cups canned pumpkin

2 tablespoons packed brown sugar

¼ teaspoon ground nutmeg

¼ teaspoon black pepper

2 bay leaves

1 cup heavy whipping cream

Cook the onions in the butter in a 4-quart Dutch oven until tender. Stir in the broth, pumpkin, brown sugar, nutmeg, pepper and bay leaves. Bring to a boil; reduce the heat. Cover and simmer for 10 minutes. Remove from the heat, and discard the bay leaves. Stir in the whipping cream.

Transfer about a third of the pumpkin mixture to a food processor or blender. Cover and process until smooth. Pour into a large bowl and continue the process until all the soup has been puréed. Return to the Dutch oven. Heat through and serve.

YIELD | 8 servings

Oregano and Parmesan-Crusted Lamb
with Roasted Shallots and Lamb Herb Jus

This is a time-consuming recipe, but it can be done in stages and is well worth the effort! Prepare the Lamb Stock and Lamb Jus the day before and refrigerate. If you buy a rack of lamb from the butcher, have the butcher remove the silver skin from the lamb and cut the rack into individual chops.

1 cup bread crumbs

2 tablespoons fresh rosemary, or
   1 tablespoon dried rosemary

1 tablespoon oregano

1 tablespoon grated Parmesan cheese

1 tablespoon minced garlic

3 tablespoons clarified butter

16 lamb chops

Kosher salt and black pepper to taste

½ cup extra-virgin olive oil

½ cup Dijon mustard

1 cup Chianti wine

1 teaspoon brown sugar

12 shallots, cut into halves

1 to 2 tablespoons extra-virgin olive oil

LAMB HERB JUS

3 cups red wine

4 cups Lamb Jus (recipe follows)

1 teaspoon finely chopped fresh thyme

1 teaspoon finely chopped fresh rosemary

Preheat the oven to 375 degrees.

Mix the bread crumbs, rosemary, oregano, Parmesan and garlic in a bowl. Add the butter and mix well.

Season the lamb chops with salt and pepper and sear in ½ cup olive oil in a heavy skillet. Remove from the skillet and let cool. Coat the outside of each chop with 1 to 2 teaspoons Dijon mustard and top with the bread crumb mixture. Roast in a large roasting pan for about 20 minutes or until the internal temperature of the lamb is 120 degrees. Remove from the oven and cover with foil. Reduce the oven temperature to 350 degrees.

Reduce the wine by half in a saucepan. Add the brown sugar and reduce by half. Sauté the shallots in 1 to 2 tablespoons olive oil in a skillet. Drizzle with the wine reduction. Sprinkle with salt and pepper. Arrange the shallots on a roasting pan and bake for 10 to 12 minutes.

For the Lamb Herb Jus, simmer the red wine in a medium saucepan until it is reduced to a syrup. Add the Lamb Jus and simmer for 10 minutes. Add the thyme and rosemary. Let stand for 10 to 15 minutes; strain through a fine sieve.

For each serving, stand 2 lamb chops upright on top of piped Truffled Gruyère Potatoes (page 29), leaning the chops against each other. Place 3 shallot halves around the potatoes and finish with the Lamb Herb Jus.

YIELD | 8 servings

LAMB STOCK

3 pounds meaty lamb bones

1 medium onion, coarsely chopped

1 rib of celery, chopped

2 shallots, peeled and chopped

3 sprigs fresh thyme

1 bay leaf

2 garlic cloves

For the Lamb Stock, bring the bones and water to cover to a boil in a large pot. Remove from the heat and discard the water. Clean the pot and rinse the bones. Return the bones to the pot and add 3 to 4 quarts fresh water. Add the onion, celery, shallots, thyme, bay leaf and garlic. Simmer for 2 ½ to 3 hours or until the broth is reduced to 6 cups. Strain through a fine sieve and refrigerate until ready to use.

LAMB JUS

2½ tablespoons olive oil

½ cup minced shallots

3 garlic cloves

¼ cup chopped fresh rosemary

2 teaspoons salt

2¼ teaspoons black pepper

Lamb Stock (recipe above)

For the Lamb Jus, heat the olive oil in a saucepan over medium heat. Add the shallots, garlic, rosemary, salt and pepper. Cook and stir for 30 seconds. Add the Lamb Stock and bring to a boil. Reduce heat to medium-low and simmer for 20 to 25 minutes or until reduced to 4 cups. Remove from the heat and strain through a fine sieve into a smaller saucepan. Heat before serving.

Truffled Gruyère Potatoes

A decadent whipped potato.

5 pounds potatoes, peeled and cut into eighths

1 tablespoon truffle salt

½ cup (1 stick) butter, melted

1 teaspoon black pepper

1 cup shredded Gruyère cheese

Milk, if needed

Boil the potatoes in a large pot of water for about 15 minutes or until tender. Drain. Add the truffle salt, butter, pepper and cheese. Whip the mixture until smooth, adding more milk if too thick.

Cover a baking sheet with parchment paper. Spoon 1 to 2 cups of the whipped potatoes into a pastry bag fitted with a large star tip. (Or use a large resealable plastic bag with a corner snipped off.) Pipe 3- to 4-inch diameter mounds of potatoes onto the parchment paper, swirling so there is a tip at the top of the circle. Potatoes may be refrigerated at this point until ready to bake.

Preheat the oven to 375 degrees. Bake the potatoes for 10 to 15 minutes or until heated through. For a browned top, broil for the last couple of minutes.

YIELD | 8 servings

Green Bean Bundles

Easy to prepare and attractive on the plate.

1½ pounds fresh green beans or haricots verts

4 thin slices ham or prosciutto, cut into ½-inch strips

2 tablespoons butter, melted

1 to 2 tablespoons brown sugar

Preheat the oven to 350 degrees.

Cook the green beans in boiling water in a saucepan until tender-crisp. Plunge immediately into ice water to stop the cooking process. Drain and pat dry.

Bundle 5 or 6 green beans and wrap with a strip of ham. Place the bundles in a buttered baking pan. Repeat with the remaining green beans and ham. Drizzle with the butter and sprinkle with the brown sugar. Bake for 10 to 15 minutes or until the green beans are warm and the brown sugar is melted.

YIELD | 6 to 8 bundles

• • •

Salad with Sautéed Pears
and Gorgonzola Cheese

This salad recipe came from the chef at Jackson's Restaurant in Pensacola, Florida.

GORGONZOLA DRESSING

6 ounces white balsamic vinegar

1½ cups Gorgonzola cheese

2 tablespoons minced garlic

1 teaspoon onion powder

Pinch of white pepper

2 teaspoons hot red pepper sauce

4 teaspoons dried parsley

2 cups olive oil

SALAD WITH SAUTÉED PEARS

10 slices bacon

2 tablespoons butter

4 tablespoons brown sugar

4 Bosc pears, peeled, quartered and cored

1 cup walnuts

Pinch of sea salt

8 cups chopped romaine lettuce

1½ cups Gorgonzola cheese

For the Gorgonzola Dressing, whisk together the vinegar, cheese, garlic, onion powder, pepper, pepper sauce and parsley in a small bowl. Add the olive oil gradually, whisking constantly.

For the Salad with Sautéed Pears, cook the bacon in a skillet until crisp; drain. Clean the skillet and add the butter and brown sugar. Sauté over medium heat for 1 minute. Add the pears and cook for 4 minutes or until light brown. Remove the pears from the pan.

Toast the walnuts in a pan for 1 to 2 minutes and sprinkle with the sea salt.

Toss the lettuce with enough Gorgonzola Dressing to coat in a bowl. Divide the lettuce among 8 salad plates. Crumble the bacon and divide it among the salad plates. Divide the cheese among the salad plates. Place 2 caramelized pear quarters on top of each salad. Sprinkle with the walnuts.

YIELD | 8 side-dish servings

Judy's Yeast Rolls

These rolls have always been a must-have at our Thanksgiving and Christmas dinners. They are too good to have only twice a year. Serve with heart-shaped butter (see Note).

1 large egg

½ cup sugar

1 teaspoon salt

2 cups lukewarm water

1 package active dry yeast

6½ to 7 cups all-purpose flour

¼ cup (½ stick) butter

Beat the egg with an electric mixer in a large bowl until foamy. Add the sugar, salt, water, yeast and 3½ cups of the flour. Beat until tiny bubbles surface and pop. Add 3 cups of the flour and mix until well blended. Add more flour if needed to make a soft dough, mixing it in by hand.

Sprinkle the counter with flour and knead the dough, adding more flour if needed to make a smooth dough ball. (My sister-in-law swears it's not necessary to knead the dough but I always do. I like the feeling of kneading dough and I think it mixes better.)

Clean the mixing bowl and grease the inside lightly. Return the dough to the bowl and cover with a clean kitchen towel. Let rise in a cold oven for 1 hour or until doubled in size. Punch down the dough.

For traditional dinner rolls, shape the dough into balls. Melt the butter in a 9 × 13-inch baking pan. Roll the dough balls in the butter and arrange them in the pan with sides touching.

For cloverleaf rolls, butter 12 muffin cups. Roll the dough into 1-inch balls and place 2 or 3 balls in each muffin cup.

Cover and allow the rolls to rise for about 1 hour.

Preheat the oven to 400 degrees. Brush the rolls with more melted butter and bake for 15 to 20 minutes or until light brown.

YIELD | 12 to 24 rolls

Note

For a special addition to these delicious rolls, use a heart-shaped butter mold to make individual butter pats. Fill the molds with softened butter and refrigerate until firm.

TIPS

PEEL EASIER | To peel hard-boiled eggs easily, cool the eggs in the water, drain the water, put the lid on the pan and shake the pan with the eggs in it. Shells will slide off easily.

CINNAMON COCOA HEART MERINGUES

Cinnamon Cocoa Heart Meringues
with Vanilla Ice Cream and Raspberry Sauce

The meringues can be made 10 days in advance.

8 large egg whites

1 teaspoon cream of tartar

2 cups sugar

8 teaspoons unsweetened cocoa powder

2 teaspoons ground cinnamon

Vanilla ice cream

Raspberry Sauce (recipe follows)

GARNISH

Fresh raspberries

Preheat the oven to 250 degrees.

Beat the egg whites with an electric mixer in a bowl until foamy. Add the cream of tartar and beat until soft peaks form. Add the sugar, ¼ cup at a time, beating until stiff peaks form. Sift the cocoa powder and cinnamon over the meringue and fold in gently but thoroughly. Transfer mixture to a pastry bag fitted with a ½-inch star tip.

Pipe 5-inch hearts onto baking sheets lined with parchment paper. Bake the meringues in the middle of the preheated oven for 1½ hours. Let cool completely on the baking sheets. Store the meringues, separated with sheets of waxed paper, in an airtight container.

When ready to serve, place a heart meringue on each plate and top with a scoop of vanilla ice cream and raspberry sauce. Garnish with raspberries.

YIELD | 8 to 10 meringues

RASPBERRY SAUCE

2 pints fresh raspberries

½ cup water

¾ cup sugar

2 tablespoons fresh lemon juice

2 tablespoons cornstarch

Combine the raspberries, water, sugar and lemon juice in a medium saucepan. Cook for 5 minutes or until the berries start to break down, stirring frequently. Press the mixture through a fine sieve. Discard the pulp. Return the raspberry mixture to the saucepan; stir in the cornstarch. Bring to a boil. Reduce the heat and simmer for 3 minutes, stirring constantly. Chill before serving. Sauce will keep in the refrigerator for up to 3 days.

TIPS

DRIP STOPPER | Stuff a mini marshmallow into the bottom of a sugar cone to stop ice cream drips.

Spinach-Stuffed Chicken in Puff Pastry
with Pink Madeira Sauce

The stuffing may be made the night before and refrigerated.

SPINACH STUFFING

6 cups chopped fresh spinach

3 cups shredded Swiss cheese

1½ cups ricotta cheese

1 large onion, finely chopped (about 1 cup)

6 hard-boiled eggs, coarsely chopped

2 large garlic cloves, crushed

2 teaspoons salt

CHICKEN AND ASSEMBLY

12 boneless skinless chicken breast halves

Salt and pepper to taste

2 (17-ounce) packages puff pastry, thawed

1 or 2 eggs, beaten

Pink Madeira Sauce (recipe follows)

For the Spinach Stuffing, combine the spinach, Swiss cheese, ricotta cheese, onion, eggs, garlic and salt in a bowl and mix well.

For the chicken, pound the chicken until thin and sprinkle with salt and pepper. (This can be done the night before. Refrigerate in a covered container.)

Spread ⅓ cup of the Spinach Stuffing over each chicken breast. Beginning at one short end, roll to enclose the filling.

Roll out the puff pastry slightly and cut enough to enclose each piece of chicken. Wrap each piece of chicken with pastry, pressing the seams to seal. Arrange 1 inch apart, seam sides down, in greased baking pans.

Preheat the oven to 400 degrees.

Cut 12 hearts from scraps of puff pastry, using a heart-shaped cookie cutter. Place a heart cutout on each chicken package. Brush lightly with beaten egg. Bake for 25 to 30 minutes or until golden brown.

To serve, drizzle some Pink Madeira Sauce on the plate and place chicken on top. Pass the remaining Pink Madeira Sauce.

YIELD | 12 servings

Note
Unbaked chicken packages may be frozen for up to 2 weeks. Freeze in a single layer until frozen and wrap securely. Defrost before baking.

• • •

Garlic Pepper Asparagus

You can use this recipe for any of your favorite fresh vegetables, such as broccoli or cauliflower.

2 pounds fresh asparagus

Olive oil

Garlic pepper

Preheat the oven to 400 degrees.

Arrange the asparagus in a single layer on a rimmed baking sheet. Coat the spears with olive oil. Sprinkle generously with garlic pepper. Bake for 8 to 10 minutes or until tender-crisp; do not overcook.

YIELD | 8 servings

PINK MADEIRA SAUCE

This sauce can be prepared a day in advance and refrigerated.

- 6 tablespoons unsalted butter
- 6 tablespoons all-purpose flour
- 6 tablespoons dry Madeira wine
- 3 cups chicken broth
- 2 tablespoons tomato paste
- 1 cup sour cream
- 1 cup chopped chives or green onion tops
- 1 teaspoon salt, or to taste
- White pepper to taste

Melt the butter in a medium saucepan. Add the flour and cook until mixture is golden brown, stirring constantly. Remove from the heat and whisk in the wine and chicken broth. Return to the heat and cook until bubbly and thickened, stirring constantly.

Mix the tomato paste and sour cream in a small bowl. Add a little of the hot wine mixture to the bowl and mix thoroughly. Return to the saucepan. Stir in the chives, salt and pepper.

If not serving immediately, place a piece of waxed paper directly on top to prevent a skin from forming. May be held at room temperature for several hours. Sauce will thicken as it stands. Reheat over low heat; do not boil. If sauce becomes too thick, thin with a little wine and sour cream in equal parts.

Yield: about 5 cups

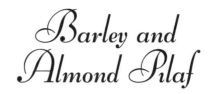

Barley and Almond Pilaf

A change from the traditional rice pilaf.

- 1 cup pearl barley
- 2 tablespoons butter
- ½ cup slivered almonds
- ¼ cup (½ stick) butter
- 1 cup diced onion
- ½ cup chopped fresh parsley
- ½ cup diced green onions
- Salt and pepper to taste
- 2 cups beef or chicken broth

GARNISH

Parsley sprigs

Preheat the oven to 375 degrees. Grease a 1½-quart baking dish.

Rinse the barley in water; drain. Melt 2 tablespoons butter in a large skillet and sauté the almonds until golden brown. Remove from the pan.

Melt ¼ cup butter in the skillet. Add the barley and onions and sauté until golden brown. Stir in the almonds, parsley, green onions, salt and pepper. Spoon into the prepared baking dish. (Recipe may be prepared to this point the day before and refrigerated.)

Bring the broth to a boil in a saucepan; pour over the barley mixture and stir to blend. Bake, uncovered, for 60 to 70 minutes or until the barley is tender and the liquid is absorbed. Garnish with parsley.

YIELD | 6 servings

Note

This recipe can be doubled successfully.

Spinach Salad

Always a favorite!

MOM'S SPINACH SALAD DRESSING

1 cup vegetable oil

1 medium onion, coarsely chopped

1 tablespoon Worcestershire sauce

½ cup sugar

⅓ cup ketchup

½ teaspoon salt

SPINACH SALAD

2 (5- to 6-ounce) packages fresh baby
   spinach leaves

4 hard-boiled eggs, chopped

8 slices bacon, cooked crisp and crumbled

1 to 2 cups fresh bean sprouts

1 (5-ounce) can water chestnuts, drained
   and chopped

For Mom's Spinach Salad Dressing, mix the oil, onion, Worcestershire sauce, sugar, ketchup and salt in a blender and blend until smooth.

For the Spinach Salad, combine the spinach, eggs, bacon, bean sprouts and water chestnuts in a large salad bowl. Toss with desired amount of salad dressing. Serve immediately.

YIELD | 8 servings

Raspberry Chocolate Cheesecake

Can be made two days before serving. Substitute a ready-made chocolate graham cracker pie shell if desired.

CHOCOLATE CRUST

1 package chocolate Nilla wafers

¾ to 1 cup butter, melted

1 tablespoon sugar

FILLING

1½ pounds cream cheese, at room
   temperature

¾ cup sugar

6 ounces bittersweet or semisweet
   chocolate, chopped and melted (do not
   use unsweetened chocolate)

¼ cup raspberry liqueur, such as Chambord

4 large eggs, at room temperature

½ cup heavy whipping cream

SOUR CREAM TOPPING

2 cups sour cream

½ cup plus 2 tablespoons sugar

2 teaspoons raspberry liqueur

1 teaspoon vanilla extract

GARNISH

1 cup whipping cream

3 tablespoons sugar

Triple Raspberry Sauce (recipe follows)

Preheat the oven to 400 degrees.

For the Chocolate Crust, process or crush the chocolate wafers finely, making 2 to 3 cups of crumbs. Mix the crumbs, butter and sugar in a bowl, adding a little more butter if needed to make the mixture stick together. Press the mixture into a 9-inch springform pan, pressing some of the crust up the side of the pan. Bake for about 5 minutes Reduce the oven temperature to 350 degrees.

For the filling, beat the cream cheese with an electric mixer in a large bowl until smooth. Add the sugar, chocolate and liqueur and mix well. Add the eggs, 1 at a time, beating just until blended. Mix in the cream until the batter is smoothly blended. Pour into the crust. Bake on the middle rack for about 55 minutes or until the center is almost set but still moves slightly when pan is shaken. Increase the oven temperature to 400 degrees.

For the Sour Cream Topping, combine the sour cream, sugar, liqueur and vanilla in a bowl and mix well. Pour over the baked cheesecake and return to the oven for about 10 minutes. Cool the cheesecake in the pan. Cover and refrigerate.

For the Garnish, whip the cream with an electric mixer. Add the sugar gradually and beat until soft peaks form.

To serve, place a slice of cheesecake on a dessert plate. Dollop a tablespoon of whipped cream onto each serving, or use a pastry bag to pipe rosettes onto the cheesecake. Pipe Raspberry Sauce hearts on the plate around the cheesecake.

YIELD | 16 to 20 servings

TRIPLE RASPBERRY SAUCE

1 cup fresh raspberries

½ cup sugar

¼ cup water

1 cup (12 ounces) seedless
  raspberry jam

1 tablespoon raspberry liqueur

Combine the raspberries, sugar and water in a small saucepan. Bring to a boil. Reduce the heat and simmer for 4 minutes, stirring frequently. Combine the raspberry mixture, jam and liqueur in the bowl of a food processor and process until smooth. Chill.

Yield: 2 cups

Soup-er Bowl Party

Comfort food at its best, soup provides an easy, fun way to party on a cold, wintery night. It's also the perfect make-ahead meal, easily adjusted for groups of all sizes. And, let's face it: it's tough to beat the combination of great soup, bread, dessert, and great friends as the ultimate relaxing and casual get-together. Have your party during the Super Bowl or hold your own separate Soup-er Bowl when the championship hype has all died away.

You can simply invite people over for soup, bread, and dessert. Nothing wrong with that! But if you want to add a little delicious rivalry to the mix, consider a Soup-er Bowl competition.

Are you ready for some FOODbowl? Great! A Soup-er Bowl party is on.

★ MENU ★

CRAWFISH AND CORN CHOWDER

INVITATION

Print the invitations on recipe cards. Mail the recipe card in an envelope or put the address on the back of the recipe card.

DECORATIONS

Use empty soup cans to hold the silverware. Feel free to leave the labels on! Large empty tin cans are a clever way to serve toppings like chips, cheese, chopped onions, etc.

ACTIVITY

A Soup-er Bowl party can be just as competitive as any football action you're watching, but far more delicious. Have people (the "cheftestants") bring a pot of their favorite soup to the party, and let guests sample the soups and vote for their favorites. Since no Super Bowl is complete without a little trash-talking, encourage friendly rivalry amongst the participants. Urge competitors to work the crowd, trying to convince people that their soup is the best and gaining votes. (But no personal fouls; that could get you ejected from the game.)

Print ballots and have people vote on their favorites, with a "Best of the Best" overall winner. Not everyone has to compete, of course. Those who don't compete can collect and count the ballots. But make sure they take their responsibilities as seriously as an NFL referee so nobody can accuse them of hometown advantage. No harm. No foul. No flag on this play!

Award prizes for the "Best of" in different categories (cream soups, chilis, healthy soups, etc.), or for categories such as "most surprising," "most creative," etc. Regardless of what you decide to call the categories, make sure you have a "Best of the Best" or "People's Choice Award" for the overall favorite.

Equipment

Extension cords and power strips for all the slow cookers

Tasting spoons

Tasting cups

Pencils

Ballots

Ask the "cheftestants" to bring their own slow cookers and soup ladles.

Prizes

The Golden Spoon for the "Best of the Best" winner: Turn an ordinary soup ladle into the soon-to-be-coveted Golden Spoon award. Use gold paint on the handle, and add as much glitz and bejeweling as you can handle. Attach the Golden Spoon to a wooden plaque or stand, adding an engraved trophy name plate indicating this year's winner. Or take the glass off a 5 × 7-inch frame, print out a page that says, "Winner: BEST OF THE BEST [year] Soup-er Bowl Competition" and then attach the ladle to the backing.

Present "Best of Category" winners with an apron, pronouncing them winner of that category. Use a computer program to assemble the winner's name plus artwork appropriate for each award. Print the image onto transfer paper and then iron it onto a plain apron for a customized apron people will be proud to wear and show off!

MENU

The following recipes include some of my favorite soups! Choose the ones that are right for your party.

Freezer Daiquiris

Ready when you are.

2 (12-ounce) cans frozen lemonade, thawed

1 (12-ounce) can frozen limeade, thawed

7 cups water

1 (750 ml) bottle rum

Stir the lemonade, limeade, water and rum together in a 1-gallon, non-glass, freezer-proof container and freeze. Stir each day. The daiquiris will be ready to serve in 48 hours. To serve, scoop into cocktail glasses and enjoy!

YIELD | 10 to 12 daiquiris

· · ·

Fried Vegetables
with Creole Mustard Sauce

For variety, experiment with different vegetables.

CREOLE MUSTARD SAUCE

⅔ cup sour cream

3 tablespoons Creole mustard

1½ teaspoons dry ranch dressing mix

1 teaspoon fresh lemon juice

½ teaspoon Creole seasoning

FRIED VEGETABLES

1 pound thick asparagus spears

2 zucchini, cut into planks

1 cup all-purpose flour

1 cup full-fat buttermilk

1 large egg

1 tablespoon hot red pepper sauce

1½ cups self-rising cornmeal mix

1 tablespoon Cajun seasoning

Peanut oil for frying

For the Creole Mustard Sauce, combine the sour cream, Creole mustard, dressing mix, lemon juice and Creole seasoning in a small bowl and mix well. Cover and chill.

For the Fried Vegetables, snap off the tough ends of the asparagus. Rinse the asparagus and zucchini with water and leave damp. Place flour in a resealable plastic bag; add the asparagus, seal and shake to coat. Repeat with the zucchini.

Whisk together the buttermilk, egg and pepper sauce in a shallow dish. Combine the cornmeal mix and Cajun seasoning in another shallow dish. Dip the vegetables in the buttermilk mixture; coat with cornmeal mixture.

Heat 2 inches of peanut oil to 365 degrees in a large Dutch oven. Fry asparagus in batches for 4 to 5 minutes or until golden brown. Drain on paper towels. Repeat with the zucchini. Serve with the Creole Mustard Sauce.

YIELD | 8 to 10 servings

Note
The vegetables can be fried in advance and heated in the oven on low before serving.

Shrimp Taco Bites

Nonstick cooking spray or olive oil spray

1 tablespoon lime juice

2 teaspoons Cajun seasoning

24 large raw shrimp, peeled and tails removed

1 large avocado, diced

1 tablespoon lime juice

½ teaspoon salt

⅓ cup sour cream

1 teaspoon finely minced chipotle peppers in adobo sauce

24 scoop-shaped tortilla chips

2 tablespoons chopped fresh cilantro

Preheat the oven to 375 degrees. Spray a baking sheet with nonstick cooking spray.

Combine 1 tablespoon lime juice and the Cajun seasoning in a medium bowl. Add the shrimp and toss to coat. Arrange the shrimp on the cookie sheet and spray lightly with the nonstick cooking spray or olive oil spray. Bake 5 to 8 minutes or until the shrimp turn pink.

Combine the avocado, 1 tablespoon lime juice and salt in a small bowl and toss to coat. Combine the sour cream and chipotle peppers in a small bowl and mix well.

Assemble the shrimp bites by placing a teaspoon of avocado mixture in a tortilla chip, followed by ½ teaspoon of sour cream mixture, then top with Cajun-lime shrimp. Sprinkle with cilantro.

YIELD | 24 bites

Vegetarian Black Bean Chili

Always nice to have for your vegetarian guests and so good, the meat eaters will love it too.

3 (15-ounce) cans black beans

1 large sweet onion, chopped

3 garlic cloves, minced

2 tablespoons vegetable oil

4 teaspoons chili powder

1 teaspoon ground cumin

½ teaspoon pepper

¼ teaspoon salt

2 (14-ounce) cans petite diced tomatoes with jalapeños, or Rotel tomatoes with chilies

1 (12-ounce) package meatless burger crumbles

1 extra large vegetable bouillon cube, or 2 regular-size vegetable bouillon cubes

2 cups water

Sour cream, shredded Cheddar cheese, sliced pickled jalapeños and diced avocados

Drain and rinse 2 cans of the black beans. Sauté the onion and garlic in hot oil in a large Dutch oven over medium-high heat 6 to 8 minutes or until tender. Stir in the chili powder, cumin, pepper and salt. Sauté for 3 minutes.

Stir in the tomatoes, meatless crumbles, bouillon cube, drained and undrained beans and water. Bring to a boil over medium-high heat. Reduce heat to medium-low and simmer for 30 minutes, stirring occasionally. Serve chili with sour cream, cheese, jalapeños and avocados.

YIELD | 10 servings

White Chicken Chili

1 pound large dried white beans

2 tablespoons olive oil

2 cloves garlic, minced

1 medium onion, chopped

1 small red bell pepper, diced

1 small green bell pepper, diced

2 (4-ounce) cans chopped green chilies

1 tablespoon ground cumin

1 tablespoon chili powder

1½ teaspoons dried oregano

¼ teaspoon ground cloves

7 cups chicken broth, plus more as needed

4 cups diced cooked chicken breast

3 cups grated Monterey Jack cheese

GARNISH

Chopped tomatoes, chopped ripe olives, guacamole, chopped green onions, sour cream, crumbled tortilla chips and salsa

Cover the white beans with water in a Dutch oven and soak overnight. Drain. Combine the olive oil, garlic, onion and bell peppers in a Dutch oven and sauté for 1 minute. Add green chilies, cumin, chili powder, oregano and cloves and sauté until onion and bell peppers are tender.

Add the chicken broth and beans and simmer, uncovered, for about 1½ hours or until the beans are tender, adding more broth as needed. Add the chicken and simmer for 1 hour longer.

Ladle into bowls and top with Monterey Jack cheese. Serve with desired garnishes.

YIELD | 8 to 10 servings

Crawfish and Corn Chowder

½ cup vegetable oil

½ cup all-purpose flour

1 onion, finely chopped

1 red bell pepper, finely chopped

1 tablespoon minced garlic

1 (17-ounce) can cream-style corn

1 (16-ounce) can whole kernel corn, drained

2 (1-pound) packages frozen crawfish tails

1 quart half-and-half

2 (11-ounce) cans tomatoes with green chilies

1 potato, peeled and chopped

1 teaspoon salt

Black pepper to taste

Cayenne pepper to taste

Whisk the oil and flour in a heavy saucepan until blended. Cook over medium-low heat until the roux is the color of peanut butter, stirring constantly. Add the onion, bell pepper and garlic and cook for 3 to 5 minutes, stirring constantly.

Add the cream-style corn, whole kernel corn and crawfish and mix well. Cook for 3 minutes, stirring frequently. Stir in the half-and-half, tomatoes, potato and salt. Cook over medium heat until the potato is tender and the chowder is thickened, stirring occasionally; do not boil. Season with black pepper and cayenne pepper.

YIELD | 10 to 12 servings

Judy's Chicken and Dumpling Soup

This is a family favorite.

1 whole chicken

1 onion, quartered

2 ribs of celery, cut into thirds

Salt and pepper to taste

3 cups all-purpose flour

1 teaspoon salt

1 egg

Place the chicken in a large Dutch oven and cover with water. Add the onion and celery. Add salt and pepper to taste. Bring to a boil and simmer for 45 minutes to 1 hour or until the chicken is tender and cooked through. Remove the chicken from the liquid and let cool.

Strain the broth, discarding the solids. Return all but 1 cup of the broth to the Dutch oven, reserving remaining 1 cup broth. Remove the chicken meat from the skin and bones, discarding the skin and bones. Cut the chicken into chunks and add to the broth.

Combine the flour, 1 teaspoon salt, egg and reserved broth in a large bowl and mix well. Knead the dough lightly on a floured surface, adding more flour if needed to make a soft nonsticky dough. Knead until smooth and elastic. Roll the dough ¼-inch thick with a rolling pin. Cut the dumplings to the desired size.

Bring the broth and chicken to a boil. Add the dumplings to the broth and simmer until they are cooked through. Add salt and pepper to taste.

YIELD | 6 to 8 servings

Crusty French Bread
with Seasoned Olive Oil Dip

CRUSTY FRENCH BREAD

1 loaf French bread

Olive oil for brushing

SEASONED OLIVE OIL DIP

1 cup good-quality extra-virgin olive oil

2 garlic cloves, pressed or minced

½ teaspoon dried oregano

½ teaspoon dried parsley

½ teaspoon dried thyme

For the Crusty French Bread, preheat the oven to 350 degrees. Brush the bread with the olive oil. Bake until crusty.

For the Seasoned Olive Oil Dip, combine the olive oil, garlic, oregano, parsley and thyme in a small bowl. Serve in dipping bowls alongside the bread.

YIELD | 1 cup dip

 TIPS

PUT OUT A FIRE | Douse a fat or oil fire with baking soda; never use water. Store a fire extinguisher in your kitchen, too.

Jalapeño Corn Bread

Add a little zip to your corn bread.

1½ cups cornmeal

1 heaping tablespoon all-purpose flour

1 teaspoon salt

½ teaspoon baking soda

1 cup buttermilk

⅔ cup vegetable oil

2 eggs, beaten

1 (14-ounce) can creamed corn

1 small green bell pepper, chopped

2 jalapeños, chopped

1½ cups grated Cheddar cheese

Preheat the oven to 375 degrees.

Mix the cornmeal, flour, salt and baking soda in a bowl. Add the buttermilk, oil, eggs and corn and mix well. Stir in the bell pepper and jalapeños and mix well.

Pour half the batter into a greased 9 × 13-inch baking pan; sprinkle with half the cheese. Repeat with remaining batter and cheese. Bake for 35 minutes or until golden brown.

YIELD | 12 servings

Lemon Ripple Ice Cream Pie

After spicy soup, an ice cream dessert makes a nice ending. The lemon curd can be made up to 3 days in advance and refrigerated. The whole pie can be made well in advance and stored in the freezer.

LEMON CURD

1 cup sugar

6 tablespoons unsalted butter, cut into small pieces

⅓ cup fresh lemon juice (about 2 lemons)

2 large eggs

2 large egg yolks

1 teaspoon grated lemon peel

ALMOND PIE CRUST

1¼ cups ground toasted almonds (about 5 ounces)

1 cup graham cracker crumbs (about 8 whole crackers)

¼ cup plus 3 tablespoons unsalted butter, melted

2 teaspoons grated lemon peel

½ teaspoon almond extract

½ gallon vanilla ice cream, slightly softened

12 ounces fresh strawberries, optional

For the Lemon Curd, combine the sugar, butter and lemon juice in the top of a double boiler over a pan of simmering water and heat until the sugar dissolves and butter melts, stirring constantly.

Beat the eggs, egg yolks and lemon peel in a bowl until well blended. Gradually whisk the warm butter mixture into the egg mixture. Return the mixture to the double boiler and cook over simmering water for about 10 minutes without boiling until the curd is thick enough to coat a spoon, stirring constantly. Test it by drawing a finger across the curd on the spoon. If your finger leaves a path that doesn't close, the curd is thick enough. Spoon the lemon curd into a bowl, whisking to smooth if necessary. Press plastic wrap directly on the surface and chill for 1 hour or until cold.

For the Almond Pie Crust, preheat the oven to 325 degrees. Butter a 9-inch springform pan. Mix the almonds, graham cracker crumbs, butter, lemon peel and almond extract in a medium bowl, stirring until the mixture is evenly moist. Press the crumbs over the bottom and 1 inch up the side of the pan. Bake for 8 minutes. Cool on a wire rack.

Spoon half the ice cream over the crust. Spoon half the curd over the ice cream. Spread with remaining ice cream. Drop tablespoons of the remaining curd over the ice cream. Use a small knife to swirl the Lemon Curd into the ice cream. Freeze for about 1 hour or just until firm. Wrap and freeze for at least 8 hours.

To serve, let the pie stand at room temperature for 10 minutes. Serve with strawberries, if desired.

YIELD | 8 to 10 servings

Blast From the Past

Military families are constantly being moved from one installation to another. That was what I loved about military life: so many memories of wonderful times at so many different locations. However, we all have times when we miss our hometowns and our families, so use this month to let your group reminisce about their childhoods and their favorite foods growing up.

My favorite childhood food was Aunt Margy's Goulash, which she made every summer at our cottage in Culver, Indiana. It was a favorite of all the cousins, and we always asked her to make it. Then there was our traditional Thanksgiving and Christmas dinner. We had the exact same menu for each holiday, and I have continued the tradition with my family. I can't imagine varying from the menu because it brings back so many wonderful family memories and it is so delicious!

★ MENU ★

POTLUCK OF FAMILY FAVORITES

49 | Classic Martinis

49 | Dirty Martinis

49 | Aunt Margy's Goulash

OUR FAMILY'S FAVORITES

50 | Stingers

50 | Hot Clam and Cheese Dip

50 | Ayre's Chicken Velvet Soup

51 | Dah's Cold Loin of Pork with Horseradish Applesauce and Mango Sauce

52 | Dah's Cheese Soufflé

53 | Overnight Layered Salad

53 | Hungarian Noodles

55 | Gingerbread with Lemon Sauce

55 | Grancy's Scalloped Oysters

56 | Wild Rice with Mushroom Gravy

SERVE WITH | Guests' Favorite Dishes

Here are a couple of options for this month. One is to host a potluck to which everyone brings a favorite childhood dish to share. Divide up the meal into categories, such as appetizers, salads, soups, main courses, side dishes, and desserts so that all courses are covered. Ask guests to bring along the recipes.

Another option is to prepare one of your family's favorite home-cooked meals for guests.

INVITATION

Shop a secondhand store or antique store for old black-and-white photographs, or use copies of your own photos. Write the invitation on the back of a photograph and mail in an envelope.

DECORATIONS

Place the photos sent by your guests around the room. Have any retro items? A lava lamp, bead curtains, yearbooks, set of encyclopedias, a high school letter jacket? Use these relics to set the scene for a "Blast from the Past!"

ACTIVITY

Before the party, ask your guests to send you a childhood picture of themselves. Number the pictures and post them around the room. As guests arrive, give each a sheet of paper listing all of the guests' names. Their task is to walk around the room attempting to match the numbered photographs with each name on the sheet. Give them a time limit for identifying the pictures. Award a prize to the person who correctly identifies the most pictures. In case of a tie, be ready with a couple of tiebreaker questions.

After all the guests have served themselves, go around the room and let everyone share a story about their dish.

Whatever option you choose for your party—potluck or your family's favorite meal—collect the recipes, copy them, and put together a "Blast from the Past" collection to give to everyone.

Classic Martinis

The less vermouth, the drier the martini—your choice.

Ice

14 ounces gin or vodka

2 ounces dry vermouth

8 pimento-stuffed olives

Chill martini glasses for 30 minutes before serving. Fill a pitcher with ice. Add the gin and vermouth and stir until the pitcher is frosty. Strain into 8 martini glasses and add an olive to each drink.

YIELD | 8 drinks

• • •

Dirty Martinis

A different twist on Classic Martinis.

8 large pimento-stuffed olives

3 ounces blue cheese

14 ounces gin or vodka

2 ounces dry vermouth

4 teaspoons olive brine

Chill martini glasses for 30 minutes before serving. Remove the pimentos from the olives and replace with the blue cheese.

Fill a pitcher with ice. Add the gin, vermouth and olive brine and stir until the pitcher is frosty. Strain into 8 martini glasses and add an olive to each drink.

YIELD | 8 drinks

Aunt Margy's Goulash

Can be made a day ahead and heated just before serving.

1¼ pounds ground beef

⅓ pound lean ground pork

1 onion, chopped

3 tablespoons Worcestershire sauce

1 (14-ounce) can whole-kernel corn, drained

2 (6-ounce) cans tomato paste

1 (3-ounce) can sliced ripe olives

1 (15-ounce) can cream of mushroom soup

8 ounces egg noodles, cooked and drained

Salt and pepper to taste

8 ounces grated sharp Cheddar cheese

Preheat the oven to 350 degrees.

Brown the ground beef, ground pork and onion in a Dutch oven, stirring to crumble. Add the Worcestershire sauce, corn, tomato paste, olives, soup, noodles, salt and pepper and mix well. Stir in half the cheese. Pour into a greased 9 × 13-inch baking dish. Top with the remaining cheese. Bake for 30 minutes or until heated through. Let stand for 5 to 10 minutes before serving.

YIELD | 8 servings

Stingers

My father and my husband drank Stingers to celebrate Bob's return from Vietnam.

Crushed Ice
8 ounces brandy
4 ounces white crème de menthe

GARNISH
Fresh mint

Fill 4 Old Fashioned glasses with crushed ice. Fill a cocktail shaker with ice; add the brandy and crème de menthe. Shake until the shaker is frosty. Strain into glasses. Garnish with fresh mint.

YIELD | 4 drinks

. . .

Hot Clam and Cheese Dip

3 tablespoons butter
1 small onion, chopped
½ cup chopped green bell pepper
1 (10-ounce) can minced clams, drained
2 tablespoons chili sauce
8 ounces processed sharp cheese, such as Old English or Kaukauna, cut into small pieces
1 tablespoon Worcestershire sauce
1 teaspoon Beau Monde seasoning
1 tablespoon Sauterne or other white wine
Dash of hot red pepper sauce
Pumpernickel bread rounds or scoop-shaped corn chips

Melt the butter in the top of a double boiler over simmering water. Add the onion and bell pepper and sauté until tender. Add the clams, chili sauce, cheese, Worcestershire, beau monde and wine. Cook until the cheese melts, stirring frequently.

To serve, spoon the dip into a heated serving dish. Serve with pumpernickel bread rounds or corn chips.

YIELD | 4 cups

. . .

Ayre's Chicken Velvet Soup

A favorite childhood trip was to Ayre's Department store in Indianapolis, which served this soup. This became our favorite soup!

¼ cup (½ stick) butter
1 cup finely diced celery
¼ cup finely diced onion
6 tablespoons butter
6 tablespoons all-purpose flour
½ cup milk
3 cups chicken broth
½ cup half-and-half
1 cup chopped cooked chicken (using a rotisserie chicken makes this easy)
1 teaspoon salt
Pepper to taste

Melt ¼ cup butter in a small saucepan. Add the celery and onion and sauté until tender.

Melt 6 tablespoons butter in a Dutch oven. Add the flour and mix well. Stir in the milk, broth and half-and-half. Add the celery and onion. Cook over medium heat until the soup boils and thickens, stirring constantly. Reduce the heat. Add the chicken, salt and pepper. Heat thoroughly. Thin with a little more milk, if needed.

YIELD | 8 (½-cup) servings

Note

This soup recipe doubles well.

. . .

Dah's Cold Loin of Pork
with Horseradish Applesauce and Mango Sauce

My grandmother's pork loin recipe, which she made for special family dinners.

1 (5- to 6-pound) pork loin, or 2 pork tenderloins

1 tablespoon dry mustard

1 tablespoon dried thyme

MARINADE

½ cup dry sherry

½ cup soy sauce

2 tablespoons grated fresh ginger, or 6 pieces candied ginger, cut into slivers

3 garlic cloves, chopped

GLAZE

8 ounces apple or currant jelly

1 tablespoon soy sauce

2 tablespoons sherry

Horseradish Applesauce (recipe follows)

Mango Sauce (page 52)

Rub the pork loin with the dry mustard and thyme.

For the Marinade, combine the sherry, soy sauce, ginger and garlic in a bowl and mix well. Pour over the pork loin. Marinate the pork in the refrigerator for 2 to 24 hours, turning frequently.

Preheat the oven to 325 degrees. Remove the pork from the marinade to a roasting pan. Insert a meat thermometer in the thickest part. Roast for about 25 minutes per pound or until the meat thermometer reaches 160 degrees, basting occasionally with the marinade.

For the Glaze, cook the jelly in a heavy saucepan over medium heat until melted and bubbly, stirring constantly. Add the soy sauce and sherry. Cook for 1 to 2 minutes, stirring constantly. Spoon over the pork and let stand for 30 minutes. Do not refrigerate. Serve with Horseradish Applesauce and/or Mango Sauce.

YIELD | 8 servings

HORSERADISH APPLESAUCE

2 tablespoons horseradish, or to taste

2 cups sweetened applesauce

Combine the horseradish and applesauce in a bowl and mix well.

Yield: 2 cups

MANGO SAUCE

2 tablespoons olive oil

1 shallot, minced

1 tablespoon minced fresh ginger

1 teaspoon curry powder

½ teaspoon fresh lemon juice

2 tablespoons mango chutney

Juice of 2 limes

⅓ cup dry Riesling or Pinot Grigio

2 mangos, peeled and diced

2 tablespoons minced cilantro

Heat the olive oil in a skillet over medium-high heat. Add the shallot, ginger, curry powder and lemon juice and sauté until the shallot is tender. Stir in the chutney, lime juice, wine and mangos. Reduce the heat and cook for 1 to 2 minutes, stirring occasionally. Remove from the heat and process in a food processor or blender until smooth, adding a little water if the sauce seems too thick. Add the cilantro. Let the sauce cool to room temperature before serving.

Yield: about 2 cups

TIPS

POTATO ERASER | Potatoes will take food stains off your fingers. Just slice and rub a raw potato on the stains and rinse with water.

Dah's Cheese Soufflé

My grandmother's most requested recipe. When she shared the recipe, she omitted the Beau Monde seasoning because she didn't want anyone else's soufflé to taste as good as hers. We could never convince her to stop doing that. This soufflé needs to stand 24 hours before baking, so plan ahead.

8 slices stale white bread

¼ cup (½ stick) butter, softened

1½ pounds grated sharp Cheddar cheese

6 eggs, lightly beaten

2½ cups half-and-half

1 rounded teaspoon brown sugar

¼ teaspoon paprika

1 shallot or green onion, finely chopped

½ teaspoon dry mustard

½ teaspoon Beau Monde seasoning

½ teaspoon salt

⅛ teaspoon cracked black pepper

½ teaspoon Worcestershire sauce

⅛ teaspoon cayenne pepper

Cut the crusts from the bread. Butter the slices well and cut into ¼-inch pieces. Butter a 9 × 13-inch baking pan. Arrange half of the bread on the bottom. Sprinkle a generous layer of cheese over it, then another layer of bread. Top with the remaining cheese.

Process the eggs in a blender for 30 seconds. Add the half-and-half, brown sugar, paprika, shallot, dry mustard, Beau Monde seasoning, salt, pepper, Worcestershire and cayenne pepper. Blend for 1 minute or until well mixed; pour over the layers, adding more half-and-half if needed to cover the bread. Cover with waxed paper. Refrigerate for 24 hours.

Remove soufflé from the refrigerator 2 hours before serving. Let stand at room temperature for 30 minutes.

Preheat the oven to 350 degrees. Place the soufflé pan in a larger baking pan. Pour cold water into the larger pan to a depth of ½ inch. Bake for 1 hour or until set.

YIELD | 8 servings

• • •

Overnight Layered Salad

Prepare this salad the day before serving. Use a large glass dish so you can see the pretty layers.

1 large head iceberg lettuce, sliced

1 large red onion, chopped

1 head cauliflower, broken into florets

1 pound bacon, fried and crumbled

¼ cup sugar

Salt and pepper to taste

2 cups full-fat mayonnaise

⅓ cup shredded Parmesan cheese

Layer the lettuce, onion, cauliflower and bacon in a large glass dish. Sprinkle with the sugar, salt and pepper. Spread with the mayonnaise, sealing to the edge. Sprinkle with the Parmesan. Refrigerate the salad for at least 8 hours. Toss just before serving.

YIELD | 8 servings

Hungarian Noodles

These noodles can be prepared early in the day. Cover and refrigerate until ready to bake.

8 ounces egg noodles

1 cup cottage cheese

2 cups sour cream

¼ cup finely chopped onion

1 garlic clove, minced

2 teaspoons Worcestershire sauce

Dash of hot red pepper sauce

½ teaspoon salt

Dash of black pepper

2 eggs, well beaten

3 tablespoons grated Cheddar cheese

Cook the noodles according to package directions; drain. Add the cottage cheese, sour cream, onion, garlic, Worcestershire sauce, Tabasco sauce, salt, pepper and eggs and mix well.

Preheat the oven to 350 degrees. Spoon the noodle mixture into a 1½-quart baking dish. Place the dish in a larger baking pan, as with a soufflé. Pour hot water into the larger pan to a depth of ½ inch. Bake for 30 minutes. Sprinkle with the cheese and bake for 10 minutes longer.

YIELD | 8 servings

GINGERBREAD WITH LEMON SAUCE

Gingerbread
with Lemon Sauce

This was my sister's favorite childhood dessert.

LEMON SAUCE

½ cup sugar

1 tablespoon cornstarch

⅛ teaspoon salt

1 cup boiling water

2 tablespoons butter

1 teaspoon lemon zest

Juice of 1 lemon

¼ teaspoon freshly ground nutmeg

GINGERBREAD

¼ cup (½ stick) butter

¼ cup shortening

½ cup sugar

2 eggs, beaten

1 cup dark molasses

2½ cups all-purpose flour

1½ teaspoons baking soda

1 teaspoon ground cinnamon

1 teaspoon ground ginger

½ teaspoon ground cloves

1 teaspoon salt

1 cup hot water

GARNISH

Whipped cream and thin lemon slices

Preheat the oven to 350 degrees. Grease an 8- or 9-inch baking pan.

For the Lemon Sauce, mix the sugar, cornstarch and salt in a saucepan. Add the boiling water. Bring the mixture to a boil. Reduce the heat and simmer until thick and transparent, stirring constantly. Stir in the butter, lemon zest, lemon juice and nutmeg.

Let the sauce cool slightly before serving.

For the Gingerbread, beat the butter and shortening in a bowl until blended. Beat in the sugar, eggs and molasses. Sift the flour, baking soda, cinnamon, ginger, cloves and salt together and add to the butter mixture. Add the hot water and beat until smooth.

Pour into the prepared pan. Bake for 35 minutes or until a knife inserted into the center comes out clean. Slice and serve with the Lemon Sauce.

YIELD | 8 to 9 servings

• • •

Grancy's
Scalloped Oysters

An unusual side dish that is great with turkey.

1 cup stale bread crumbs

2 cups butter cracker crumbs, such as Waverly Wafers

1 cup (2 sticks) butter, melted

1 quart standard oysters, cut into halves if large

Salt and pepper to taste

½ cup oyster liquid

¼ cup heavy cream

Preheat the oven to 450 degrees.

Drain oysters, saving the liquid. Mix the bread and cracker crumbs; stir in the butter. Cover the bottom of 7 × 11-inch glass baking dish with a layer of crumb mixture. Cover with a layer of oysters. Sprinkle with salt and pepper. Add another layer of crumbs, oysters and seasoning. Cover with remaining crumbs. Drizzle oyster liquid and cream over the top. Bake, uncovered, for 30 minutes.

YIELD | 6 to 8 servings

Wild Rice
with Mushroom Gravy

My favorite recipe from my mom.

1 small onion, finely chopped

1 to 2 cups finely chopped celery

¼ cup (½ stick) butter

3 tablespoons all-purpose flour

½ cup milk

3 cups cooked wild rice

½ teaspoon salt

¼ teaspoon sage

⅛ teaspoon thyme

⅛ teaspoon pepper

Mushroom Gravy (recipe follows)

Preheat the oven to 350 degrees.

Brown the onion and celery in the butter until tender; stir in flour. Add milk gradually and cook, stirring, until it is thickened. Add the cooked wild rice, salt, sage, thyme and pepper and mix well. Spoon the mixture into a large, buttered baking dish. Bake for 20 to 25 minutes until hot. Serve with Mushroom Gravy. This recipe can be easily doubled.

YIELD | 8 to 10 servings

Note

Grancy's Scalloped Oysters and Wild Rice with Mushroom Gravy are some of our family's favorite holiday recipes. They are delicious any time of the year.

Mushroom Gravy

This all-purpose gravy is great on any food that might benefit from gravy. It is wonderful over Thanksgiving turkey. This recipe doubles easily and can be made in advance and reheated.

2 cups sliced fresh mushrooms

3 tablespoons butter

3 tablespoons all-purpose flour

1½ cups milk, or ¾ cup milk and
 ¾ cup turkey or chicken broth

½ teaspoon salt

Dash of nutmeg

Dash of black pepper

2 egg yolks

1 to 2 teaspoons lemon juice, or to taste

Melt the butter in a skillet over medium heat. Brown the mushrooms in the butter until almost tender. Sprinkle the flour over the mushrooms a little at a time, stirring to moisten the flour after each addition. Add the milk, salt, nutmeg and pepper and mix well. Cook until thickened, stirring constantly. Reduce the heat.

Beat the egg yolks in a bowl. Pour 1 cup of the hot mushroom mixture into a separate bowl. Add the egg yolks gradually to the hot mixture, beating constantly. Return the egg mixture to the skillet. Add the lemon juice and cook for 2 minutes, stirring constantly.

YIELD | 2 cups

Happy Chinese New Year!

With January 1st having come and gone, you may be feeling a post-holiday letdown. With Chinese New Year, there is more holiday fun in store for you. (And for this New Year, you don't even have to make any resolutions!)

Chinese New Year is celebrated to bring good luck and prosperity in the year ahead—a perfect excuse to throw a party! Depending on the Chinese lunar calendar, the fifteen-day celebration begins in either late January or early February. Even in March, this party is still fun, festive, and incredibly tasty—what else could you want in a party? And, after all, who doesn't want more luck and prosperity in their life?

A traditional Chinese New Year celebration culminates with a colorful Lantern Festival. Can you imagine a more spectacular party setting than a room full of glowing lanterns? And with Chinese food so popular, people will undoubtedly enjoy the food as much as the celebration.

★ MENU ★

INVITATION

Enclose an invitation inside a homemade fortune cookie (recipe follows). Place the fortune cookie in a Chinese takeout container. Another idea is to write your invitation on colorful red paper and fold like a fan.

DECORATIONS

Red decorations are traditional. Red, the color of fire, symbolizes good fortune and joy. Each year of the Chinese calendar is symbolized by one of twelve zodiac animals, so use this year's animal as a focal point of your decoration, centerpieces of flower arrangements, etc. Lanterns are a must. You can make your own or find them online. Orange stems and leaves symbolize family branches, so decorate with orange branches. If you can't find them, then fill a bowl with oranges and surround it with leaves. Dragons, firecrackers, and chopsticks are also great decorating ideas.

ACTIVITY

Chopstick Race. Before the race, give everyone time to practice with chopsticks. For the race, prepare bowls of food in various size pieces. Start with a larger food like marshmallows and then progress to smaller items such as candies, nuts or beans, and then, finally, rice. Have couples compete against other couples to see who can lift the items, one at a time, into their bowls without dropping them.

FAVORS AND PRIZES

Money in a red envelope is a traditional Chinese New Year gift. An even number of bills is considered lucky. Chocolate coins are another possibility. Bags of gummy fish symbolize abundance. Since red symbolizes luck, give red candies as prizes or favors.

THE FOOD

At a Chinese New Year party, special foods are served that either symbolize wealth and prosperity or resemble items associated with wealth and prosperity. Here are some examples:

- Egg rolls look like gold bricks and represent prosperity.
- Shrimp dishes symbolize happiness for the coming year.
- Chinese marble tea eggs represent prosperity.
- A whole fish symbolizes togetherness and abundance.

My father was stationed in Thailand for two years, and we all learned to love Chinese food. We had a Chinese cook who taught my mother wonderful Chinese dishes. I have included some of these in this menu.

Fortune Cookies

This is a time-consuming process but is worth the "wows" you will receive from your invitees. Before making the fortune cookies, write your invitations on strips of paper. Fold them so they are ready to tuck into the warm cookies. It's important to work quickly when shaping the fortune cookies.

4 large egg whites, at room temperature
1 cup superfine sugar
1 cup all-purpose flour, sifted
Pinch of salt
5 tablespoons unsalted butter
½ teaspoon almond extract
½ teaspoon vanilla extract
Nonstick cooking spray
3 tablespoons water

Combine the egg whites and sugar in a medium bowl. Beat with an electric mixer for 1 to 2 minutes or until frothy. Add the flour and salt and beat until well mixed. Add the butter, almond extract and vanilla extract and beat for 30 seconds or until mixed.

For each cookie, spray a small skillet with cooking spray. Add 1 tablespoon of the batter, tilting the skillet to spread the batter into a thin circle. Cook for 4 to 7 minutes or until the edges turn brown. Turn the cookie and cook until brown. Remove the cookie from the skillet.

Working quickly, dab water along the top arch of the cookie. Fold the cookie to form a taco shape, pressing the top arch to seal and leaving the sides open. Slide an invitation strip inside, making sure a bit of the invitation sticks out. Insert an index finger into each open side and press your thumbs gently into the center while bringing the open ends toward each other, forming the shape of a fortune cookie. Place the cookie on a wire rack to cool.

Place one fortune cookie in a small Chinese carryout container filled with tissue paper or other filler. Seal and deliver to your invitees their very own edible invitations.

YIELD | 12 to 15 cookies

. . .

Lychee Martinis

Canned lychees are available in the Asian section of most grocery stores.

Ice cubes
6 ounces vodka
4 ounces lychee juice
Splash of vermouth

GARNISH
2 lychees

Fill a cocktail shaker with ice. Add the vodka, lychee juice and vermouth. Shake until chilled. Pour into 2 martini glasses and garnish with lychees.

YIELD | 2 drinks

. . .

Egg Rolls

A recipe from my mother.

1 pound ground pork
1 to 2 tablespoons sesame oil
4 green onions, finely chopped
1 clove garlic, minced
½ cup finely chopped celery

1 cup diced cooked fresh shrimp (or canned)

¾ cup shredded cabbage or bagged cabbage slaw mixture

1 (5-ounce) can water chestnuts, drained and finely chopped

¼ to ½ cup soy sauce

1 package egg roll wrappers

Peanut oil

Sweet-and-Sour Sauce (page 65)

Chinese mustard

Cook the ground pork in the sesame oil in a skillet until slightly cooked, stirring to crumble. Add the green onions, garlic and celery and cook until ground pork is cooked through. Add the shrimp, cabbage and water chestnuts. Add enough soy sauce to flavor all the ingredients but not make the mixture soupy. Cook over low heat to incorporate the soy sauce into the shrimp mixture.

For each egg roll, place an egg roll wrapper on a work surface in a diamond shape. Spoon about 1 heaping tablespoon of the mixture onto the center of each egg roll wrapper. Fold up the bottom corner of the egg roll to cover the filling. Fold the left corner over the filling and then fold in the right corner. Brush the top corner with a little water. Roll up the egg roll and press the top corner to seal. Place on a baking sheet covered with parchment paper.

Heat 2 inches of peanut oil in a 2-quart saucepan to 350 degrees. Fry the egg rolls a few at a time in the hot peanut oil—do not crowd the pan. Fry until golden brown. Drain on paper towels. Serve with Sweet-and-Sour Sauce and Chinese mustard.

If not serving immediately, cool the egg rolls, wrap in plastic wrap and freeze. When ready to serve, heat on a baking sheet at 350 degrees.

YIELD | 18 to 20 egg rolls

Hot Sour Soup

6 ounces lean boneless pork

4 ounces fresh shiitake mushrooms, stems removed, caps thinly sliced, or dried shiitake mushrooms, soaked and sliced

1 to 2 tablespoons vegetable oil

6 cups chicken broth

1 (8-ounce) can bamboo shoots, drained

1 (3-ounce) can sliced mushrooms, drained

½ pound medium-firm tofu, drained

3 tablespoons vinegar

2 tablespoons soy sauce

½ teaspoon salt

½ teaspoon red pepper flakes

2 tablespoons cornstarch

4 tablespoons water

1 egg, beaten

GARNISH

4 green onions, finely chopped

Place the pork in the freezer for 15 to 30 minutes for easier slicing. Slice the pork into ¼ × 2-inch strips. Heat the oil in a 3-quart saucepan. Cook the pork and shiitake mushrooms in the hot oil until the pork is lightly browned; drain.

Add the broth to the saucepan. Bring to a boil. Add the pork mixture, bamboo shoots, canned mushrooms and tofu. Simmer for 5 minutes. Add the vinegar, soy sauce, salt and pepper flakes. Blend the cornstarch and water in a small cup; stir into the soup. Cook, stirring frequently, until slightly thickened and bubbly. Pour the beaten egg slowly into the bubbly soup. Cook for 1 to 2 minutes longer, stirring frequently. Garnish with the green onions.

YIELD | 6 servings

Egg Foo Yung

One of my mother's favorite recipes.

BROWN SAUCE

2 tablespoons cornstarch

3 cups cold chicken bouillon or broth

2 teaspoons soy sauce

½ teaspoon sugar

Freshly ground pepper

EGG PANCAKES

3 to 4 ounces dried black mushrooms

6 eggs

3 cups chopped cooked chicken (I buy a rotisserie chicken)

2 green onions, chopped

½ cup finely chopped celery

1 (5-ounce) can sliced water chestnuts, drained and chopped (or chopped water chestnuts, chopped into smaller pieces)

½ to ¾ cup fresh or drained canned bean sprouts

Salt and pepper to taste

6 tablespoons vegetable oil

Preheat the oven to 350 degrees.

For the Brown Sauce, mix the cornstarch with ½ cup of the bouillon in a small saucepan. Add the remaining bouillon, soy sauce, sugar and pepper. Bring to a boil over medium heat. Reduce the heat and simmer until thickened, stirring constantly.

For the Egg Pancakes, soak the mushrooms in very hot or boiling water in a bowl for 20 minutes; drain and squeeze dry. Slice into thin strips.

Beat the eggs lightly in a medium bowl. Add the chicken, mushrooms, green onions, celery, water chestnuts, bean sprouts, salt and pepper. Mix gently.

Heat the oil in a large skillet. Spoon ¼-cup portions of the egg mixture into the skillet to make small pancakes. Cook until lightly browned. Turn the pancakes and cook until the egg is set.

Arrange the pancakes in a 9 × 13-inch baking dish, overlapping if necessary. Top with the Brown Sauce. Bake for 15 to 20 minutes.

YIELD | 8 servings

Note

This dish can be made ahead of time. Store the sauce and pancakes separately, covered, in the refrigerator. Pour the sauce over the pancakes in the baking dish just before baking. Bake at 350 degrees for about 30 minutes.

• • •

Fried Rice

An easy and delicious dish from my father. It can be used as a side dish or as a main dish.

1 to 2 tablespoons toasted sesame oil

3 eggs, lightly beaten

1½ pounds ground pork

¼ cup chopped onion

1 to 2 cups soy sauce

7 to 8 cups cooked white rice

GARNISH

1 seedless cucumber, thinly sliced

6 green onions, chopped

Heat 1 tablespoon of the sesame oil in a large skillet over medium-high heat. Add the eggs and scramble until cooked through. Remove the eggs from the skillet and set aside. Add a little more sesame oil to the skillet and add the ground pork and onion. Cook until pork is cooked through, stirring to crumble.

Add 1 cup of the soy sauce and cook the pork mixture for about 3 minutes to incorporate the soy sauce into the pork. Stir in the cooked rice in stages, stirring in additional soy sauce as needed.

Stir in the scrambled eggs just before serving. Transfer to a serving platter and garnish with the cucumber and green onions. Serve with hot red pepper sauce and additional soy sauce.

YIELD | 8 servings

• • •

Chow Mein
over Crispy Noodles

My niece always chooses this dish for her birthday dinner.

1 pound sirloin steak

1 tablespoon cornstarch

½ cup water

6 tablespoons soy sauce

4 ounces thin Chinese noodles

1 cup vegetable oil

2 teaspoons grated ginger

1 large onion, thinly sliced

2 ribs of celery, chopped

½ cup fresh mushrooms, thinly sliced

1 cup water chestnuts, drained and thinly sliced

1 package fresh pea pods

Slice the steak into strips. Dissolve the cornstarch in the water and soy sauce in a small bowl.

Cook the noodles in 6 cups of boiling water until softened but not done. Drain and rinse with cold water.

Heat the oil in a skillet. Add the noodles and fry for 1 to 2 minutes or until crispy; drain. Remove to a baking sheet; keep warm in the oven.

Discard all but 3 tablespoons of the oil. Sauté the ginger until fragrant. Add the steak and cook through. Remove the steak from the skillet. Sauté the onion, celery, mushrooms, water chestnuts and pea pods until tender-crisp. Return the steak to the skillet. Add the soy sauce mixture and cook, stirring constantly, until the sauce thickens and coats the meat and vegetables. Serve on top of the crispy noodles.

YIELD | 8 servings

Note

The Chinese noodles may be placed in a single layer on a greased baking sheet and baked in a 375-degree oven for 15 to 20 minutes or until crisp, turning once.

 TIPS

SCORCH AWAY | If there is burnt food on your pan, add a drop or two of dish soap and enough water to cover the bottom of the pan. Bring to a boil on the stovetop.

Kung Pao Chicken

KUNG PAO SAUCE

2 tablespoons soy sauce

2 tablespoons rice wine or dry sherry

2 tablespoons unseasoned rice vinegar

3 tablespoons hoisin sauce

2 teaspoons toasted sesame oil

CHICKEN

1½ tablespoons cornstarch

1 large egg white, lightly beaten

1½ tablespoons soy sauce

1 pound boneless skinless chicken breasts, cut into 1-inch cubes

6 green onions

3 tablespoons peanut oil

2 teaspoons red pepper flakes, or to taste

1 tablespoon finely grated peeled fresh ginger

2 cloves garlic, minced

½ cup unsalted roasted peanuts

For the sauce, whisk the soy sauce, rice wine, rice vinegar, hoisin sauce and sesame oil in a small bowl and set aside.

For the chicken, whisk the cornstarch, egg white and soy sauce in a medium bowl. Add the chicken and toss to coat. Refrigerate for 30 minutes.

Slice the green onions very thinly, keeping the green tops and white bottoms separate.

Set a wok over high heat. Add the peanut oil and heat through. Add the pepper flakes, ginger, garlic and the white bottoms of the green onions; stir-fry for about 30 seconds. Remove the chicken from the marinade and add to the wok; stir-fry for 1 to 2 minutes or until golden brown. Add the sauce and cook until heated through. Top with the peanuts and serve.

YIELD | 8 servings

Crispy Shrimp
with Sweet-and-Sour Sauce

Serve as an appetizer or as part of the main course.

SHRIMP AND MARINADE

1 egg, lightly beaten

1 tablespoon cornstarch

1 teaspoon dry white wine

1 teaspoon soy sauce

1 pound fresh shrimp, shelled and deveined

COATING AND FRYING

Peanut oil for frying

½ cup all-purpose flour

½ cup water

3 tablespoons cornstarch

1 tablespoon vegetable oil

½ teaspoon baking soda

½ teaspoon salt

Sweet-and-Sour Sauce (recipe follows)

To marinate the shrimp, mix the egg, cornstarch, wine and soy sauce in a bowl. Add the shrimp. Cover and refrigerate for 10 minutes.

To coat and fry the shrimp, heat 2 inches of peanut oil in a saucepan to 375 degrees. Mix the flour, water, cornstarch, vegetable oil, baking soda and salt in a medium bowl and mix well. Remove the shrimp from the marinade. Add the shrimp to the flour mixture and stir to coat. Fry the shrimp in batches for 2 to 3 minutes or until golden brown—do not crowd the pan. Drain. Serve hot with Sweet-and-Sour Sauce.

YIELD | 8 servings

Note

The fried shrimp can be covered and refrigerated for up to 2 hours and reheated in a 450-degree oven for about 10 minutes.

SWEET-AND-SOUR SAUCE

⅓ cup red wine vinegar

½ cup ketchup

⅓ cup sugar

⅓ teaspoon hot red pepper sauce

Mix the wine vinegar, ketchup, sugar and pepper sauce in a small bowl. Stir to dissolve the sugar.

Yield: about 1 cup

Spicy Green Beans

1½ pounds fresh green beans, trimmed

¼ cup soy sauce

2 cloves garlic, minced

2 teaspoons garlic chili sauce

2 teaspoons honey

4 teaspoons canola oil

Cook the green beans in boiling water in a saucepan for 3 to 4 minutes or until tender-crisp.

Mix the soy sauce, garlic, chili sauce and honey in a small bowl.

Heat the canola oil in a skillet over medium heat. Add the green beans and stir-fry for 3 to 5 minutes. Stir in the soy sauce mixture. Cook for 2 minutes or until the liquid is nearly evaporated, stirring constantly. Serve immediately.

YIELD | 8 servings

FRIED BANANA WONTONS AND FRIED WONTON KISSES

Fried Banana Wontons with Honey

6 bananas

1 package egg roll wrappers

Peanut oil for frying

Confectioners' sugar

½ to 1 cup honey

Peel the bananas and cut into quarters.

For each wonton, place an egg roll wrapper on a work surface in a diamond shape. Place a banana quarter on the bottom corner and roll the banana in the wrapper to enclose, folding in the sides and dabbing with water to seal as you roll. Leave the top tip of the diamond exposed.

Heat 5 to 6 inches of peanut oil to 375 degrees in a saucepan. Fry the wontons until golden brown; drain on paper towels. Sprinkle with confectioners' sugar. Drizzle with the honey just before serving.

YIELD | 24 wontons

• • •

Fried Wonton Kisses

24 chocolate kisses, unwrapped

24 wonton wrappers

Vegetable oil for frying

Confectioners' sugar

For each wonton, place a chocolate kiss in the center of a wonton wrapper. Moisten the edges of the wrapper with water. Bring the opposite corners together over the chocolate kiss and press to seal.

Heat 2 inches of oil to 375 degrees in a Dutch oven. Fry the wontons in batches for 2 to 2½ minutes or until golden brown, turning once; drain on paper towels. Sprinkle with confectioners' sugar.

YIELD | 24 wontons

• • •

Hot Buttered Rum

Not exactly Chinese, but this is a great after-dinner drink. Keep in the freezer to have on hand when a different after-dinner drink is called for.

1 pound brown sugar

1 pound confectioners' sugar

1 pound butter, softened

1 quart vanilla ice cream, softened

Butter

Hot water

Rum

Combine the brown sugar, confectioners' sugar and softened butter in a mixing bowl and beat until creamy. Add the ice cream and mix well. Spoon into a freezer-safe container and freeze.

To serve, place 2 tablespoons butter, 1 cup hot water and a shot of rum in a cup. Add a heaping tablespoon of the ice cream mixture. Stir and enjoy!

YIELD | about 20 drinks

Spring into Spring

Spring is a favorite time of year! The weather is getting warmer and the birds wake you up even before the alarm sounds. There is an energy that says, "IT'S SPRING!" Channel that energy by thinking about gardening. There is nothing like having your own garden. A yard of beautiful blooming flowers or a patch of fresh vegetables is the "gift that keeps on giving." You can have a home filled with freshly cut flowers or enjoy homegrown vegetables all year round.

INVITATION

Buy packets of flower and vegetable seeds. Write the invitation on a sticky label and adhere it to one side of each seed packet. Use another sticky label to address the invitation and put it on the opposite side of the seed packet. Mail the entire seed packet. You can place the seed packet inside an envelope, if you prefer, and mail the envelope.

DECORATIONS

Bring out your bright spring items, such as pastel tablecloths and napkins. Use branches of blooming forsythia or cherry blossoms for a beautiful and fragrant centerpiece. Or ask your guest speaker to donate flowers or plants from the nursery to use as centerpieces. Use the centerpieces as giveaways at the end of the party.

ACTIVITY

For a spring gathering, bring in an expert from your local nursery for a demonstration on planting techniques for your area. Composting has become very popular and is a great way to be environmentally friendly. Be sure to include composting techniques in the discussion. Since not everyone has a yard suitable for a garden, "container gardening" could be a useful topic.

Another idea is developing a community garden. Many neighborhoods have an area set aside for a community garden. Do some research to see if there is one in your area. If so, a group could get organized and share a garden plot. Since there are endless ideas for a gardening talk, choose your guest speaker based on what would best suit the needs and desires of your guests.

★ MENU ★

Tropical Martini

3 parts pineapple rum

1 part apricot nectar

½ part cream of coconut

½ part banana liqueur

¼ part lime juice

Ice

GARNISH

Grated coconut

Sprig of mint

Combine the rum, apricot nectar, cream of coconut, banana liqueur and lime juice in a martini shaker filled with ice. Shake until well chilled and strain into a martini glass. Rim the glass with grated coconut and garnish with a sprig of mint.

YIELD | 1 drink

Raspberry Mojitos

Make the Raspberry Simple Syrup 24 hours before serving. The syrup can be stored in the refrigerator for up to 2 weeks.

RASPBERRY SIMPLE SYRUP

1 cup sugar

1 cup water

2 cups raspberries

MOJITOS

8 (¼-inch) lime slices (about 2 limes)

8 fresh mint leaves

4 ounces Raspberry Simple Syrup

1 cup white rum

¼ cup raspberry liqueur

¼ to ½ cup Sprite or Squirt

Ice cubes

GARNISH

Sprigs of mint

Raspberries

For the Raspberry Simple Syrup, combine the sugar and water in a small saucepan. Cook over medium heat until the sugar dissolves. Remove from the heat and add the raspberries. Allow the mixture to steep for at least 24 hours.

For 2 Mojitos, muddle or crush 4 lime slices and 4 mint leaves in a cocktail shaker. Add 2 tablespoons of the Raspberry Simple Syrup, ½ cup of the rum, and ⅛ cup of the raspberry liqueur to the mixture. Add ice, cover and shake. Strain into 2 mojito or rock glasses filled with ice. Top off with Sprite or Squirt. Repeat the directions to make 2 additional mojitos. Garnish each with a sprig of mint and a raspberry.

YIELD | 4 drinks

Tomato Bocconcini Salad
in a Martini Glass

A pretty presentation for a great salad. A variety of colors of cherry tomatoes is always nice.

½ cup extra-virgin olive oil

½ cup balsamic vinegar

1 garlic clove, crushed

1 teaspoon sugar

Salt and pepper to taste

8 ounces baby bocconcini, cut into halves

1 pint cherry tomatoes, cut into halves

½ cup chopped fresh basil

GARNISH

Chopped fresh basil

Combine the olive oil, vinegar, garlic, sugar, salt and pepper in a jar and shake to blend.

Arrange a combination of bocconcini, tomatoes and basil in each martini glass. Sprinkle with the olive oil mixture. Garnish with basil.

YIELD | 6 servings

SUGAR SOFTENER | Place a slice of apple in a bag of hardened brown sugar to soften the brown sugar.

She-Crab Soup

¼ cup (½ stick) butter

¼ cup olive oil

1 onion, chopped

1 fennel bulb, chopped

4 ribs of celery, chopped

2 carrots, chopped

4 garlic cloves , minced

¼ cup all-purpose flour

2 tablespoons tomato paste

1 teaspoon salt

1 teaspoon black pepper

½ cup dry sherry

5 cups clam juice

¼ cup chopped fresh parsley

1 tablespoon chopped fresh tarragon

2 cups heavy cream

2 pounds fresh crabmeat, drained and sorted

Melt the butter with the olive oil in a Dutch oven over medium heat. Add the onion, fennel, celery, carrots and garlic and sauté for 8 minutes or until tender. Stir in the flour and cook for 1 minute. Add the tomato paste, salt, pepper, sherry and clam juice gradually, stirring constantly. Stir in the parsley and tarragon.

Bring the mixture to a boil. Reduce the heat and simmer, uncovered, for 15 minutes or until reduced to 4 cups. Purée in batches in a food processor or blender. Return the soup to the Dutch oven; stir in the cream. Cook over medium-high heat for 25 minutes or until thickened. Add the crabmeat and cook for 3 to 5 minutes or until warmed through.

YIELD | 9 cups

CURRIED CHICKEN CANAPÉS

Curried Chicken Canapés

The pastry cups can be made a day ahead and stored in an airtight container.

Nonstick cooking spray

1 package phyllo dough, thawed

⅔ cup mayonnaise

2 tablespoons sour cream

Zest of 1 lemon

2 teaspoons lemon juice

1 tablespoon curry powder

1 teaspoon Beau Monde seasoning

Salt and pepper to taste

⅓ cup finely chopped celery

4 green onions including green tops, chopped

⅓ cup finely chopped red bell pepper

1 (5-ounce) can sliced water chestnuts, coarsely chopped

1 tablespoon minced fresh cilantro

3 or 4 boneless skinless chicken breast halves, cooked and finely diced, or 1 rotisserie chicken, finely diced

GARNISH

½ cup shredded coconut, lightly toasted

Cilantro

Preheat the oven to 375 degrees. Spray muffin cups with nonstick cooking spray.

Spray 1 sheet of phyllo with cooking spray. Top with a second sheet and spray with cooking spray. Cut into 4-inch squares. Place a square in a muffin cup, pressing gently into the cup. Add 3 more 2-ply squares to the cup, rotating each slightly to make "petals." Repeat to make 24 cups. Bake for 8 to 10 minutes or until golden brown. Let stand to cool.

Combine the mayonnaise, sour cream, lemon zest, lemon juice, curry powder and Beau Monde seasoning in a bowl and mix well. Stir in the salt, pepper, celery, green onions, bell pepper, water chestnuts, cilantro and chicken and mix well.

Spoon a small amount of the chicken mixture into each phyllo cup. Garnish with toasted coconut and a sprinkle of cilantro.

YIELD | 24 canapés

SMELLS GONE | Quell the smell in your refrigerator's vegetable drawer by lining it with newspaper.

Key Lime Pie
with Grand Marnier Whipped Cream

A refreshing end to a great party.

KEY LIME PIE

2½ cups finely crushed graham crackers

⅓ cup sugar

½ cup (1 stick) unsalted butter, melted

½ teaspoon almond extract

2 teaspoons unflavored gelatin

4 tablespoons cold water

4 egg yolks

1 cup fresh key lime juice

2 (14-ounce) cans sweetened condensed milk

GRAND MARNIER WHIPPED CREAM

½ pint heavy whipping cream, well chilled

2 tablespoons sugar

1 tablespoon Grand Marnier liqueur

GARNISH

Lime wheels

Preheat the oven to 350 degrees.

For the Key Lime Pie, combine the cracker crumbs, sugar, butter and almond extract in a small bowl and mix well. Press into a 9- or 10-inch pie pan. Bake for 10 minutes or until golden brown. Let stand to cool.

Soften the gelatin in the water and stir to dissolve.

Combine the egg yolks and lime juice in a heavy saucepan. Cook over medium heat for 10 minutes or until slightly thickened; do not boil. Whisk in the softened gelatin. Let stand to cool or place the saucepan in a large bowl filled with ice to cool.

Whisk the condensed milk into the cooled mixture and stir until well blended and thickened. Spoon the mixture into the crust and spread evenly. Cover with plastic wrap and refrigerate.

For the Grand Marnier Whipped Cream, combine the cream, sugar and liqueur in a mixing bowl. Beat with an electric mixer on high until stiff peaks form. Refrigerate until ready to use.

Top each slice of pie with Grand Marnier Whipped Cream and garnish with a lime wheel.

YIELD | 6 to 8 servings

 TIPS

WAX ON LINENS | To remove candle wax from linens, wait for the wax to dry, then pick off what wax you can with your fingernails. Put the cloth in the freezer for several days so the wax will stiffen. Once it is hardened, scrap off with a kitchen knife. Place paper towels on the top and bottom sides of the stain and press with a warm iron. It may be necessary to change the paper towels several times to absorb all the wax. Launder as you normally would.

Game Night

Many of us grew up playing games. Whether they are board games, card games or a combination of the two, it is fun to gather your friends for a little friendly competition. A Game Night is an easy party to put together, and you can individualize it for the games that you like to play. It is important to choose games that are easy to explain and play. It is also important to have a menu that you can prepare ahead of time so that you can enjoy the games along with your guests.

Drinks and appetizers are offered as your guests arrive. Then they draw a number out of a bowl; the number corresponds with a number on one of the card tables. This will be the table where they will begin. We have found that it is easiest if you choose games that can be played by groups of four. Set up card tables throughout your house, depending on the number of games you are playing. We normally had 16 guests and would set up 4 numbered card tables.

INVITATION

Glue the invitation to the backside of a playing card. Place the card in an envelope and mail it to your invitees. Write on the invitation for them to bring the card with them to the party. (It will be used for one of your games.)

ACTIVITY

As your guests enjoy some appetizers and drinks, explain the games and the scoring. Give everyone a score sheet listing the games and a space for their score. They then go to the table corresponding to the number they drew. Set a timer for 15 minutes. After 15 minutes the games stop and each player gets a score of 1 to 4. The player with the top score receives 4 points; the 2nd top scorer receives 3 points, the 3rd top scorer receives 2 points, and the lowest scorer receives 1 point. Each player writes their score on their score sheet and moves to the next table. At the end of the four games, the scores are totaled and a prize is given to the top winner. If there is a tie, you could cut playing cards to determine the winner; the player with the highest card is the winner.

At the end of the night, ask your guests to pull out the invitations they brought with them. For fun, play a quick game of 5-card poker. Dealer deals out 4 cards; guests use the cards on their invitations as the 5th card. The highest poker hand wins. Have a prize for the winner.

★ MENU ★

SERVE WITH | French bread from the store or bakery

SOME SUGGESTIONS FOR GAMES

Farkle

Players roll six dice with the goal of reaching the highest score using a combination of numbers on the dice. Farkle can be purchased at most stores that sell toys. The directions are easy to follow.

Scrabble

Players keep track of the points they receive for each word they put on the board.

Monopoly

Players count up Monopoly money at the end of the game. Houses are worth $100; hotels are worth $500.

Memory

A game from your childhood. Arrange all 52 playing cards facedown on the table. Players take turns turning up 2 cards. If a match is made, the player may continue to turn up 2 cards. Each player keeps track of the pairs they find.

Bushwacker

4 ounces cream of coconut

2 ounces Kahlúa

1 ounce dark rum

1 ounce crème de cacao

4 ounces half-and-half

2 cups ice cream

Combine the cream of coconut, Kahlúa, rum, creme de cacao, half-and-half and ice cream in a blender; blend until well mixed.

YIELD | 1 drink

Note

May substitute 2 cups crushed ice for the ice cream.

. . .

Crawfish Beignets

2 eggs

½ cup milk

8 ounces crawfish tails

1 tablespoon Cajun seasoning

¼ cup finely chopped green bell pepper

¼ cup finely chopped green onions

¼ cup finely chopped celery

1 tablespoon finely chopped garlic

2 ears roasted corn, cut off the cob, or 1 cup corn kernels

1½ cups all-purpose flour

1 teaspoon salt

1 teaspoon baking powder

Vegetable oil for deep frying

Honey or rémoulade (optional)

Beat the eggs well in a large bowl. Add the milk, crawfish, Cajun seasoning, bell pepper, green onions, celery, garlic and corn. Mix well. Add the flour, salt and baking powder and gently mix until flour is incorporated.

Heat the oil to 350 degrees in a deep fryer. Drop the crawfish mixture by small scoopfuls or tablespoonfuls into the hot oil. Fry in small batches for 7 to 10 minutes. Remove and drain on paper towels; season with salt. Drizzle with honey or serve with your favorite rémoulade, if desired.

YIELD | 24 beignets

. . .

Party Meatballs

May be made ahead and frozen or refrigerated.

2½ pounds ground beef

2 eggs

¼ cup water

1 cup bread crumbs

1 small onion, finely chopped

⅛ teaspoon pepper

1 (16-ounce) can whole berry cranberry sauce

1 (12-ounce) bottle chili sauce

2 tablespoons brown sugar

1 tablespoon lemon juice

1 package frozen cheese tortellini (optional)

Preheat the oven to 350 degrees. Combine the ground beef, eggs, water, bread crumbs, onion and pepper in a bowl and mix well.

Shape into 1-inch meatballs. Bake on a rimmed baking sheet for 15 minutes or until cooked through.

Combine the cranberry sauce, chili sauce, brown sugar and lemon juice in a large saucepan and mix well. Simmer until the sauce is hot. Transfer the meatballs to the sauce and simmer for 1 hour.

Add a package of tortellini to the sauce 10 minutes before serving, if desired. Serve in a crockpot or chafing dish.

YIELD | 15 to 20 appetizers

• • •

Chutney Cheese Round

The cheese mixture freezes well.

  6 ounces cream cheese, softened
  1 cup grated Cheddar cheese
  ½ teaspoon curry powder
  ½ teaspoon garlic powder
  ¼ teaspoon salt
  4 teaspoons dry sherry
  4 ounces Major Grey's Chutney, chopped
  ½ bunch green onions including green
    tops, chopped
  Crackers

Combine the cream cheese, Cheddar cheese, curry powder, garlic powder, salt and sherry in a bowl and mix well. Shape the mixture into a flat 5- to 6-inch circle. Wrap in plastic wrap and refrigerate for flavors to meld.

Remove from the refrigerator about 2 hours before serving. Top with the chutney and green onions. Serve with crackers.

YIELD | 6 to 8 servings

Stuffed Mushrooms

The mushrooms may be stuffed, covered and refrigerated 1 day before serving.

  6 slices bacon
  ½ onion, chopped
  1 garlic clove, minced
  4 ounces feta cheese
  ¼ teaspoon red pepper flakes
  ¼ cup finely chopped walnuts or pecans
  20 to 30 white or portobello mushrooms,
    1½ inches in diameter, stemmed
  Olive oil

Preheat the oven to 375 degrees.

Fry the bacon in a skillet until crisp; drain on paper towels. Coarsely crumble the bacon. Drain all but ¼ cup bacon grease from the skillet; add the onion and cook until almost tender. Add the garlic and cook for 1 to 2 minutes. Transfer the onion and garlic to a bowl; mix in the bacon, feta cheese, pepper flakes and nuts.

Toss the mushrooms with a little olive oil in a bowl. Arrange the mushrooms round side up on a rimmed baking sheet. Bake for 10 minutes. Turn the mushrooms over and fill with the bacon mixture, mounding slightly on top. Bake for 10 to 12 minutes or until heated through.

YIELD | 20 servings

Blue Cheese Salad
with Balsamic Vinaigrette and Spicy Pecans

SPICY PECANS

⅓ cup sugar

¼ cup (½ stick) butter

¼ cup orange juice

1¼ teaspoons salt

1¼ teaspoons cinnamon

¼ teaspoon ground red pepper

4 cups pecan halves (about 1 pound)

BALSAMIC VINAIGRETTE

½ cup balsamic vinegar

3 tablespoons Dijon mustard

3 tablespoons honey

2 garlic cloves, minced

1 shallot, minced

1 cup olive oil

Salt and pepper to taste

BLUE CHEESE SALAD

16 ounces salad greens

1 (4-ounce) package blue cheese, crumbled

2 oranges, peeled and sliced

1/2 cup sliced fresh strawberries

For the Spicy Pecans, preheat the oven to 250 degrees. Combine the sugar, butter, orange juice, salt, cinnamon and red pepper in a heavy skillet over medium heat. Heat until the butter melts and the sugar dissolves, stirring constantly. Remove from the heat; add the pecans and toss to coat. Line a baking sheet with foil and spread the pecans over the foil. Bake for 1 hour, stirring every 15 minutes. Store in an airtight container.

For the Balsamic Vinaigrette, whisk together the vinegar, mustard, honey, garlic and shallot in a small bowl. Add the olive oil slowly, blending well. Add salt and pepper.

For the Blue Cheese Salad, toss the salad greens, cheese, oranges and strawberries with the Balsamic Vinaigrette. Top with the Spicy Pecans.

YIELD | 6 servings

TIPS

REVIVE HONEY | Revive crystallized honey by placing the glass jar in simmering water in a frying pan. Stir the honey until the crystals have dissolved. Don't store honey in the refrigerator. It can last forever once opened because enzymes in bees' stomachs create by-products that fight bacteria.

BLUE CHEESE SALAD WITH BALSAMIC VINAIGRETTE AND SPICY PECANS

Seafood Lasagna

May be made a day ahead and refrigerated before baking.

1 green onion, finely chopped

1 cup sliced mushrooms

2 to 3 tablespoons butter

½ cup chicken broth

1 (8-ounce) bottle clam juice

1 pound bay scallops

1 pound uncooked small shrimp, peeled and deveined

8 ounces fresh crabmeat, or frozen crabmeat

⅛ teaspoon white pepper

½ cup (1 stick) plus 2 tablespoons butter

½ cup all-purpose flour

1½ cups milk

½ teaspoon salt

⅛ teaspoon white pepper

1 cup heavy whipping cream

¼ cup shredded Parmesan cheese

9 lasagna noodles, cooked and drained

GARNISH

Chopped parsley and green onion

Preheat the oven to 350 degrees. Grease a 9 × 13-inch baking pan.

Sauté the green onion and mushrooms in 2 to 3 tablespoons butter in a large skillet until tender. Stir in the broth and clam juice; bring to a boil. Add the scallops, shrimp, crabmeat and ⅛ teaspoon white pepper; return to a boil. Reduce the heat and simmer, uncovered, for 4 to 5 minutes or until the shrimp turn pink and the scallops are firm and opaque, stirring gently. Drain, reserving the liquid.

Melt ½ cup plus 2 tablespoons butter in a large saucepan and stir in the flour until smooth. Combine the milk and reserved cooking liquid in a small bowl; gradually add to the flour mixture. Add the salt and ⅛ teaspoon white pepper. Bring to a boil and cook for 2 minutes or until thickened, stirring constantly. Remove from the heat; stir in the cream and ¼ cup cheese.

Stir ¾ cup of the sauce into the seafood mixture. Spread ½ cup of the sauce in a greased 9 × 13-inch baking pan. Top with 3 noodles, spread with half the seafood mixture and 1¼ cups of the sauce. Repeat noodle, seafood and sauce layers. Top with the remaining noodles and sauce. Sprinkle with ¼ cup cheese. Bake, uncovered, for 35 to 40 minutes or until golden brown and bubbly. Let stand for 15 minutes before cutting. Garnish with parsley and green onion.

YIELD | 12 servings

Beef Lasagna

This delicious dish looks complicated, but it is not. The meat sauce is great over spaghetti as well.

1 pound ground beef

2 tablespoons olive oil

1 onion, chopped

3 garlic cloves, minced

1 shallot, minced

2 tablespoons dried oregano

2 tablespoons dried parsley

1 tablespoon dried basil

1 teaspoon dried rosemary

1 teaspoon salt

½ teaspoon pepper

1 tablespoon sugar

2 (6-ounce) cans tomato paste

1 (28-ounce) can tomato sauce

1 (28-ounce) can diced tomatoes

3 cups ricotta cheese or cottage cheese

2 eggs, beaten

1 tablespoon dried parsley

1 teaspoon salt

½ teaspoon pepper

3 cups grated mozzarella cheese

1 cup freshly grated Parmesan cheese,

9 lasagna noodles, cooked and drained

Cook the ground beef in the olive oil in a large skillet over low heat until lightly browned. Add the onion, garlic and shallot and cook until the ground beef is thoroughly browned and the onion, garlic and shallot are tender. Add the oregano, 2 tablespoons parsley, basil, rosemary, 1 teaspoon salt, ½ teaspoon pepper and sugar and mix well. Add the tomato paste, tomato sauce and undrained diced tomatoes gradually and mix well. Reduce the heat and simmer the meat sauce for 30 minutes to 1 hour, stirring occasionally.

Preheat the oven to 375 degrees. Grease a 9 × 13-inch baking pan.

Mix the ricotta cheese, mozzarella cheese, eggs, 1 tablespoon parsley, 1 teaspoon salt and ½ teaspoon pepper in a small bowl.

Spread ½ cup of the meat sauce over the bottom of the baking pan. Top with 3 noodles. Spread one third of the ricotta mixture over noodles. Repeat the meat sauce, noodle and ricotta mixture layers twice more. Add the remaining meat sauce and top with the mozzarella and Parmesan cheeses. Bake, uncovered, for 30 to 40 minutes or until browned and bubbly. Cool for 10 minutes before cutting.

YIELD | 12 servings

 TIPS

GOODBYE GREASE | Getting rid of excess grease in a pan after cooking ground beef or bacon can be messy. Simply drop a piece of bread or two into the pan to soak up the grease, then discard the bread.

Crème de Menthe Cake

An easy make-ahead dessert.

- 1 (18-ounce) package white cake mix
- ¼ cup green crème de menthe
- 1 (12-ounce) chocolate fudge sauce
- 1 (16-ounce) container whipped topping
- 3 tablespoons green crème de menthe

GARNISH

Chocolate curls

Preheat the oven according to the package directions.

Prepare the cake batter according to the package directions, adding ¼ cup crème de menthe and mixing well. Bake in a 9 × 13-inch baking pan according to the package directions. Let stand to cool.

Spread fudge sauce over the cooled cake. Combine the whipped topping and 3 tablespoons crème de menthe and mix gently. Spread over the fudge sauce. Garnish with chocolate curls.

YIELD | 16 servings

TIPS

FLOUR PANS | When a recipe says to flour the pan, use a little bit of the dry cake mix instead—no more flour on the outside of the cake.

Chocolate Caramel Pecan Cheesecake

A friend gave me this recipe 15 years ago, and it is still a favorite!

- 2½ cups finely crushed Oreos
- ½ cup (1 stick) butter, melted
- 1 (10-ounce) package caramels
- 5 ounces evaporated milk
- 1½ cups pecans, coarsely chopped
- 3 (8-ounce) packages cream cheese, at room temperature
- ¾ cup sugar
- 3 eggs
- 1½ cups chocolate chips, melted
- 1½ teaspoons vanilla extract

Preheat the oven to 350 degrees.

Combine the crushed Oreos and butter in a bowl and mix well. Press over the bottom of a 10-inch springform pan. Bake for 10 minutes. Let the crust cool to room temperature.

Melt the caramels with the milk in a small saucepan. Pour over the crust. Sprinkle with the pecans, distributing them evenly over the caramel.

Beat together the cream cheese and sugar in a bowl. Beat in the eggs, melted chocolate and vanilla. Pour over the prepared crust. Bake for 55 to 65 minutes or until the center is set. Chill completely before serving.

YIELD | 16 to 20 servings

Kentucky Derby

You don't have to live in Kentucky to go the Kentucky Derby—hold your own! We held one when we were stationed at Fort Riley, Kansas, and we had a ball!

Our "racetrack" was the parade field in front of our home, but a yard could be used just as easily. We kept it very simple: two poles in the ground were the "starting gate." And two more were the "finish line." Both had ropes strung between them. Participants paired up, with one person as the "jockey" and the other as the "horse." The jockey jumped on the back of the horse, and they were ready to go. The team that broke through the finish line first, won.

Keep the track short, because it is not easy to carry an adult on your back for a very long distance. Our group was big, so we worked in heats. The winner of each heat ran in the final "Kentucky Derby." The winner received a "rose" garland made from red tissue paper and plastic greenery. (You could use plastic roses from the craft store.) We also purchased a trophy with a plaque so that we could engrave the winning team's name on it and use it yearly.

INVITATION

I ordered Derby glasses and placed an invitation inside each glass and hand-delivered it. Another choice is to make a nice invitation using a template of jockey silks, which can be found online.

DECORATIONS

There are many great websites for Kentucky Derby decorations. Plan ahead and order them after the Kentucky Derby to take advantage of sales on jockey silks, balloons, and other items.

ACTIVITY

Teams should choose a name and number. We made up betting sheets ahead of time and inserted the names and numbers of the horses and jockeys. Use Monopoly money for betting on the races. Offer prizes for first-, second-, and third-place winners.

Hats are a "must" at the Kentucky Derby, so hold a hat contest! Give a prize for the most original hat.

MENU

I have included two asparagus recipes—a knife-and-fork recipe and a pick-up recipe. Choose the one that best suits your party.

★ MENU ★

Mint Juleps

You can't have a Derby party without Mint Juleps! Prepare the mint syrup 12 to 24 hours before serving.

MINT SYRUP

2 cups sugar

2 cups water

1 cup (about) fresh mint sprigs

JULEPS

1 cup fresh mint sprigs

Crushed ice

2 to 3 ounces good-quality Kentucky bourbon per drink

For the Mint Syrup, combine the sugar and water in a saucepan. Bring to a boil and boil for 5 minutes without stirring. Cool completely before using. Fill a jar loosely with the mint and add the cooled syrup. Refrigerate for 12 to 24 hours. Strain into a pitcher, discarding the mint.

For each Julep, spoon ½ tablespoon of the Mint Syrup into a julep cup. Add 1 mint sprig and fill with crushed ice. Pour in 2 to 3 ounces of bourbon. Sip through a straw to capture the full aroma of the mint.

YIELD | 8 servings

Iced Tea Sangria

Refrigerate for several hours or make the night before.

SIMPLE SYRUP

1 cup sugar

1 cup water

SANGRIAS

4 family-size tea bags

4 cups boiling water

2 cups red or white wine

2 cups chopped oranges, mangos and strawberries

GARNISH

Lemon and lime wheels

For the Simple Syrup, combine the sugar and water in a saucepan. Bring to a boil and boil for 5 minutes without stirring. Cool completely before using.

For the Sangrias, steep the tea bags in the boiling water in a pitcher for 5 minutes. Remove the tea bags, squeezing to release any excess tea and discarding the bags. Combine the tea, wine and ½ to ¾ cup of the Simple Syrup. Refrigerate for several hours or make the night before.

For each Sangria, spoon about ¼ cup chopped oranges, mangos and strawberries into a glass and add sangria. Float lime and lemon wheels in the pitcher of remaining sangria.

YIELD | 8 servings

Note

The Simple Syrup may be stored in the refrigerator for up to 2 weeks.

Chive Biscuits with Ham

2½ cups all-purpose flour

2 teaspoons baking powder

1 teaspoon salt

½ cup plus 2 tablespoons shortening

1 tablespoon chopped fresh chives

¾ cup buttermilk

1½ to 2 pounds thinly sliced country ham

Preheat the oven to 375 degrees.

Sift together the flour, baking powder and salt into a bowl. Cut in the shortening until the mixture resembles coarse meal. Add the chives. Stir in buttermilk to make a soft dough. Knead on a lightly floured surface until smooth and elastic. Roll to 1-inch thickness and cut into 1½-inch circles. Arrange on a lightly buttered baking sheet. Bake for 15 minutes.

Cut each biscuit horizontally into halves. Add a portion of ham between the layers. Arrange on a serving platter.

YIELD | 24 biscuits

• • •

Asparagus with Bourbon Sauce

This side dish is a knife-and-fork affair for seated parties.

48 fresh asparagus spears (about 2½ pounds)

½ cup (1 stick) butter

½ cup chopped pecans

½ cup 80-proof bourbon

Trim asparagus of any woody stems. Steam or boil for 4 to 5 minutes or until bright green and tender-crisp; drain. Plunge immediately into ice water; drain and refrigerate until just before serving time.

Melt the butter in a large skillet. Add the pecans and toast lightly. Add the bourbon and boil just until the alcohol cooks away. Add the asparagus and heat through.

YIELD | 8 servings

Note

You can also combine all of the ingredients in a covered baking dish and bake in a 250-degree oven until heated through.

• • •

Country Ham and Asparagus Wraps

Unbaked wraps can be frozen for up to 1 month. Ask your butcher to slice the country ham for you.

1 (17-ounce) package puff pastry

1 egg, beaten

2 tablespoons water

16 ounces country ham, very thinly sliced

16 ounces thin asparagus spears

16 ounces Swiss cheese, thinly sliced

1 cup full-fat mayonnaise

2 tablespoons mustard

Thaw the pastry at room temperature for 30 minutes but do not unwrap until ready to use. Unfold the pastry on a lightly floured surface. Roll each sheet into a 10 × 14-inch rectangle and cut into 1 × 10-inch strips. Beat the egg with the water in a small bowl. Brush each strip with the egg mixture.

Preheat the oven to 400 degrees.

Tear the ham into 3 × 3-inch pieces. Cut the asparagus to measure about 4 inches. Slice the cheese into ¼- to ½-inch strips.

Wrap a piece of cheese and then a ham slice around an asparagus spear. Wrap a pastry strip around the ham, slightly overlapping the pastry. Arrange on ungreased baking sheets. Bake for 12 to 18 minutes or until the pastry is golden brown.

Combine the mayonnaise and mustard in a small bowl. Serve as dip with the wraps.

YIELD | 28 to 30 wraps

• • •

Cheese Grits

1 cup quick-cooking grits

2 cups milk

⅓ pound Cheddar cheese, shredded

½ cup (1 stick) butter

2 eggs, lightly beaten

2 garlic cloves, minced

1 teaspoon salt

Pinch of white pepper

Pinch of ground nutmeg

Preheat the oven to 350 degrees. Grease a 9-inch baking dish.

Cook the grits according to package directions, substituting 2 cups milk for the water. Remove from the heat. Add the cheese and butter and cook until the cheese is melted, stirring constantly. Add the eggs, garlic, salt, pepper and nutmeg and mix well.

Pour the mixture into the prepared baking dish. Bake for 25 to 30 minutes or until set.

YIELD | 8 to 10 servings

• • •

Bourbon Balls

12 ounces vanilla wafers, finely crushed (about 3 cups)

1 cup finely chopped pecans

½ cup confectioners' sugar

1 cup semisweet chocolate morsels

½ cup light corn syrup

⅓ cup Maker's Mark bourbon, or other good-quality Kentucky bourbon

½ cup confectioners' sugar

Stir together the wafer crumbs, pecans and ½ cup confectioner's sugar in a medium bowl.

Melt the chocolate morsels with the corn syrup in a saucepan. Add the bourbon and cook until smoothly blended, stirring constantly. Pour the chocolate mixture over the crumb mixture and stir to mix thoroughly.

Shape the mixture into 1-inch balls. Place on waxed paper. Roll balls in ½ cup confectioners' sugar in a shallow bowl. Place on waxed paper in a container or in small paper candy cups. Store in an airtight container for about 3 days before serving. These will keep for up to 2 weeks.

YIELD | 48 balls

TRIPLE CROWN PIE

Triple Crown Pie

A triple treat: chocolate, pecans and bourbon!

2 eggs, at room temperature

¾ cup sugar

½ cup dark corn syrup

2 tablespoons butter

½ teaspoon vanilla extract

Pinch of salt

⅓ cup bourbon

1 (9-inch) unbaked pie shell

4½ ounces pecans, chopped

½ cup chocolate chips

Bourbon Whipped Cream (recipe follows)

Preheat the oven to 350 degrees.

Beat the eggs with an electric mixer on high speed in a 1-quart bowl until fluffy and lemon colored. Beat in the sugar gradually. Reduce the speed to low. Add the corn syrup, butter, vanilla, salt and bourbon and mix well.

Pour the mixture into the pie shell. Sprinkle with the pecans and chocolate chips. Bake for 40 minutes or until the crust is golden brown. Serve warm with Bourbon Whipped Cream.

YIELD | 6 to 8 servings

BOURBON WHIPPED CREAM

1 cup heavy whipping cream

2 tablespoons sugar

1 tablespoon good-quality Kentucky bourbon

Combine the cream, sugar and bourbon in a bowl. Whip with an electric mixer on high speed until stiff peaks form.

Yield: 1 cup

 TIPS

FRESH EGG OR NOT? | To determine whether an egg is fresh, immerse it in a pan of cool salted water. If it sinks, it is fresh. If it rises to the surface, throw it out.

Great Finds Pizza Party

Great Finds Pizza Party is a fun party I heard about from a friend. Her daughter and friends have had several of these parties over the years. The party grows larger each year as friends hear about it and want to be included in this fun way to find new beauty products and secrets and share them.

Send out invitations to your girlfriends for a Great Finds Pizza Party. Ask invitees to wrap and bring their favorite beauty product/secret that costs $25 or less. Also ask them to bring their favorite appetizer, sweet treat or bottle of wine to share. Everyone leaves with a gift and several beauty tips and ideas.

★ MENU ★

95 | Tangerine Cosmopolitans

95 | Hot Party Ryes

95 | Pizza Sauce

96 | Pizza Dough

97 | Alfredo Sauce

97 | Fruit Pizza

CHOICE OF PIZZA TOPPINGS | sausage, pepperoni, chicken, fresh spinach, onion, bell peppers, mushrooms, anchovies, black olives, tomatoes, Cheddar cheese, mozzarella cheese, goat cheese, feta cheese, smoked salmon

INVITATION

Find one of those "miracle product" ads in a magazine or look online for "miracle beauty products" and find a fun ad. Print it out, and use the other side of the paper to write up your invitation. Be sure your invitation explains the party and what the guests need to bring. The invitation sent by my friend was worded like this: "You are invited to the 5th Annual Beauty Party Gift Exchange where you leave with not only a great gift but also tons of new ideas for beauty products and secrets. Please bring your favorite beauty product/secret (wrapped and under $25). Please bring either an appetizer, sweet treat or bottle of wine to share. Let me know whether you will be bringing an appetizer, sweet treat or a bottle of wine when you RSVP."

DECORATIONS

No need for any fancy decorating ahead of time for this party. All you will need is a table to hold the wrapped beauty products and a table for the appetizers, sweet treats, and wine. The pizza bar can be set up on the counters in your kitchen.

ACTIVITY

As guests arrive, they discreetly place their wrapped gifts on the gift table. Allow time for everyone to mingle, get a bite to eat and something to drink. Guests pick a number out of a basket for the gift exchange. The person with #1 picks out a gift and opens it. The person who brought that gift explains why it is a favorite product and how they use it. For example, one guest brought hand lotion and explained that the lotion was her favorite because it made a huge difference in the condition of her hands when used nightly. She then told where to buy it.

The gift exchange continues with #2, who can either take the gift that was just opened or choose one from the table. This continues until everyone has a gift. Gifts can only be stolen twice.

As gifts are opened and explained, the hostess takes notes on all the details. After the party, the host sends the guests an email that lists the products that were brought, a brief explanation of the products and where they can be purchased.

To add extra fun to the evening, include a make-your-own pizza bar. After the gifts have been opened and exchanged, open up the pizza bar, where you have pizza dough and bowls of pizza toppings and sauce. Guests make pizzas for themselves by rolling out the amount of dough they want for their pizza and topping it with their desired toppings. You can have individual pizza pans or use baking sheets that hold two or three individual pizzas each.

Tangerine Cosmopolitans

3 cups orange tangerine juice

1½ cups vodka

¼ cup triple sec

Ice cubes

GARNISH

Thin orange wheels

Combine the juice, vodka, triple sec and ice in a pitcher; stir well. Pour into chilled martini glasses. Garnish with orange wheels.

YIELD | 6 drinks

• • •

Hot Party Ryes

Great appetizer to freeze and have on hand for unexpected guests.

1 pound pork sausage (preferably Jimmy Dean)

1 pound ground beef

1 pound Velveeta

1 tablespoon Worcestershire sauce

1 teaspoon garlic salt

2 loaves party rye bread

Preheat the oven to 350 degrees.

Brown the sausage and ground beef in a skillet, stirring to crumble. Drain well on paper towels. Add the Velveeta, Worcestershire sauce and garlic salt. Cook until the Velveeta is melted, stirring frequently. Spread about 1 tablespoon of the mixture on each bread slice, using about 1½ loaves of the bread. Arrange the ryes on a baking sheet and bake for 10 to 15 minutes or until hot and bubbly.

YIELD | 60 appetizers

Note

To bake at a later time, arrange party ryes on a baking sheet, cover and freeze. When frozen, remove from the baking sheet, place in a resealable plastic bag and place in the freezer. To reheat, arrange on a baking sheet and bake at 375 degrees for 15 to 20 minutes or until hot and bubbly.

• • •

Pizza Sauce

2 tablespoons olive oil

½ cup finely chopped onion

¼ cup finely chopped celery

1 garlic clove, minced

1 (28-ounce) can crushed tomatoes

1 (6-ounce) can tomato paste

1 teaspoon dried oregano

1 teaspoon dried basil

½ teaspoon salt

½ teaspoon sugar

¼ teaspoon pepper

1 bay leaf

Heat the olive oil in a medium skillet. Add the onion, celery and garlic and sauté until tender. Add the tomatoes, tomato paste, oregano, basil, salt, sugar, pepper and bay leaf and mix well. Simmer over low heat for 1 hour, stirring occasionally. Remove the bay leaf. May be left chunky or puréed in a blender or food processor until smooth.

YIELD | about 4 cups

Pizza Dough

¾ cup warm water

1 envelope active dry yeast (about 1½ teaspoons)

1 tablespoon olive oil

1 teaspoon salt

1¾ cups all-purpose flour, divided

Yellow cornmeal

Preheat the oven to 500 degrees.

Pour the water into a large bowl. Sprinkle the yeast over water and stir to blend. Let stand for 10 minutes or until the yeast is foamy. Add the olive oil and salt and mix well. Add 1½ cups of the flour and mix until a sticky dough forms.

Knead the dough on a floured surface until smooth and elastic, adding just enough flour to keep the dough from sticking to the surface. Shape the dough into a ball and place in a large, greased bowl. Turn to coat. Cover and let rise at room temperature for 2 hours or until almost doubled. Punch dough down and shape into a ball. Return to the bowl and cover. Let rise for 3 hours or until doubled in volume. Punch dough down and shape into a ball. Cover until ready to use.

Roll the dough into a 13-inch circle. Sprinkle cornmeal on a baking sheet and place the rolled pizza dough on top of the cornmeal. Build your pizza by spreading with sauce and adding desired toppings. Cook for 15 to 20 minutes or until the pizza is cooked through.

YIELD | dough for 1 (13-inch) pizza

Alfredo Sauce

¼ cup (½ stick) butter

1 garlic clove, crushed

8 ounces cream cheese, chopped

1 cup heavy whipping cream

1½ cups grated Parmesan cheese

¼ teaspoon white pepper

½ cup chopped fresh parsley

Melt the butter in a medium saucepan. Add the garlic and sauté for 1 to 2 minutes. Add the cream cheese. Cook until the cream cheese is melted, stirring constantly. Add the cream, Parmesan and pepper. Cook until the Parmesan is melted and the mixture is well blended, stirring constantly. Stir in the parsley.

YIELD | about 1½ cups

Fruit Pizza

A light, easy, make-ahead dessert in keeping with the pizza theme.

PIZZA

1 (8-ounce) package refrigerated sugar cookie dough

8 ounces whipped cream cheese, at room temperature

1 tablespoon sugar

Fresh or canned pineapple, cut into bite-size pieces

Seedless grapes, cut into halves or quarters

Strawberries, cut into bite-size pieces

Kiwi, cut into bite-size pieces

Bananas, cut into bite-size pieces

Fruit or berries of choice

ORANGE GLAZE

½ cup orange marmalade

1 tablespoon water

Preheat the oven to 375 degrees.

Press the cookie dough over a foil-lined 14-inch pizza pan. Bake for 10 to 12 minutes or until golden brown. Cool. Remove the foil; place the crust on a serving platter.

Beat the cream cheese and sugar in a mixing bowl until smooth; spread over the cookie crust. Arrange the pineapple, grapes, strawberries, kiwi and bananas on top of the cream cheese mixture.

For the Orange Glaze, combine the orange marmalade and water in a small bowl and mix well.

Spoon the Orange Glaze over the fruit. Cut the pizza into wedges.

YIELD | 8 to 10 servings

Flag Day

Flag Day normally goes unnoticed in June, overshadowed by Father's Day and upcoming Fourth of July. Flag Day is a great way to begin your summer and get a jump on the patriotic spirit.

In the United States, Flag Day, celebrated on June 14, commemorates the adoption of the U.S. flag, in 1777 by resolution of the Second Continental Congress. In 1916, President Woodrow Wilson issued a proclamation that officially established June 14 as Flag Day.

The United States Army also celebrates the Army's birthday on this date, so if you are connected to the Army you could have a dual celebration: Flag Day and an Army birthday party.

INVITATION

Print an American flag on cardstock. Two flags will fit on an 8½ × 11-inch piece of cardstock. Print the invitation on the back of the flag. Cut the flag into large jigsaw pieces, put them in an envelope, and mail them to your guests. They will need to put the pieces together to read their invitations.

DECORATIONS

Let red, white, and blue reign! This is the party for bringing out the sparklers, flags, and all your patriotic decorations. Make it simple and use paper products. Find them on sale after the Fourth of July and stock up. This is a great picnic-style party to take outside. Fire up your grill and set up tables outside. It is PICNIC TIME!

ACTIVITY

Place state flags around the room. You can print state flags and put them on stands or you can go online and order miniature state flags from miniatureflagshop.com for a very reasonable price.

Develop state trivia questions and post them around the room. (Include some Army trivia in your posters if you decide to celebrate the Army birthday as well.) Give each couple an answer sheet for them to identify as many state flags as they can and answer the trivia questions. Award a patriotic prize to the couple with the highest score.

★ MENU ★

SERVE WITH | Potato salad from the deli or homemade

Easy Frozen Margaritas

A refreshing drink for a patriotic picnic.

1 (6-ounce) can frozen limeade concentrate, thawed

¾ cup gold tequila

½ cup orange liqueur, such as triple sec

4 to 6 cups ice cubes

¾ cup gold tequila

¼ cup orange liqueur, such as triple sec

1 (6-ounce) can frozen pineapple juice concentrate, thawed

3 medium limes, quartered

Combine the limeade concentrate, ¾ cup tequila, and ½ cup orange liqueur in a blender. Fill the blender almost to the top with ice. Blend on high speed until thick and slushy. Transfer to a pitcher.

Combine ¾ cup tequila, ¼ cup orange liqueur and pineapple juice concentrate in the blender. Fill the blender almost to the top with ice. Blend on high speed until thick and slushy. Add to the pitcher with the limeade mixture and mix well. Serve in margarita glasses, squeezing fresh lime juice on top of each drink.

YIELD | 12 margaritas

Taco Tartlets

These tartlets can be frozen and reheated before serving.

1 pound ground chuck

2 teaspoons taco seasoning mix

2 tablespoons ice water

1 cup sour cream

2 ounces black olives, chopped

2 tablespoons taco sauce

¾ cup crushed corn chips or tortilla chips

1 cup shredded Cheddar cheese

Preheat oven to 425 degrees.

Mix the ground beef, taco seasoning mix and ice water in a bowl with your hands. Press small amounts of the mixture into mini muffin cups to form shells.

Combine the sour cream, olives, taco sauce and crushed chips. Spoon a little of the filling into each muffin cup, mounding slightly. Sprinkle with equal portions of the cheese. Bake for 7 to 9 minutes. Loosen and remove the tartlets from the muffin cups using a knife. Serve warm.

YIELD | 30 to 36 tartlets

 TIPS

MORE JUICE | To get the most juice out of fresh lemons or limes, bring them to room temperature and roll them on the counter before squeezing.

Coconut Shrimp

These are best served hot, so consider setting up the fryer outside and frying the shrimp in front of your guests.

1½ cups all-purpose flour

⅔ cup beer

½ teaspoon baking powder

½ teaspoon paprika

½ teaspoon curry powder

¼ teaspoon salt

¼ teaspoon cayenne pepper

½ cup all-purpose flour

2 cups shredded sweetened coconut

2 pounds medium to large shrimp with tails intact, peeled and deveined

Vegetable oil for deep frying

Orange Horseradish Sweet-and-Sour Sauce (recipe follows)

Combine 1½ cups flour, beer, baking powder, paprika, curry powder, salt and cayenne pepper in a bowl and mix well.

Spread ½ cup flour on a plate or in a shallow bowl. Place the coconut in a bowl.

Coat the shrimp with flour and then dip into the batter to coat all but the tail. Coat with the coconut.

Heat the oil to 350 degrees in a deep fryer. Fry the shrimp in batches for 1 to 2 minutes or until the coconut is golden brown. Drain on paper towels. Serve with Orange Horseradish Sweet-and-Sour Sauce.

YIELD | 12 servings

ORANGE HORSERADISH SWEET-AND-SOUR SAUCE

1 (18-ounce) jar orange marmalade

3 tablespoons Creole mustard

2 to 3 tablespoons prepared horseradish

Combine the orange marmalade, Creole mustard and horseradish in a small bowl and mix well.

Yield: 1¼ cups

Dry Ribs

These are my husband's favorite ribs.

1 tablespoon cumin

2 teaspoons chili powder

1 teaspoon seasoned salt

¼ teaspoon cayenne pepper

2 tablespoons lemon juice

2 racks baby back pork ribs

Mix the cumin, chili powder, seasoned salt and cayenne pepper in a small bowl. Sprinkle both sides of the ribs with the lemon juice and the cumin mixture. Wrap with aluminum foil and refrigerate until ready to grill.

Preheat the grill to medium-high.

Remove the ribs from the foil and grill for 15 to 20 minutes on each side.

YIELD | 6 to 8 servings

Barbecued Ribs

This was my grandmother's recipe, and we all loved it!

BARBECUE SAUCE

1 onion, chopped

¼ cup vegetable oil

1 cup ketchup

½ cup water

¼ cup packed brown sugar

¼ cup lemon juice

3 tablespoons Worcestershire sauce

2 tablespoons prepared mustard

1 teaspoon salt

¼ teaspoon hot red pepper sauce

RIBS

2 racks baby back pork ribs

2 lemons, sliced

1 onion, cut into rings

Preheat the oven to 425 degrees.

For the Barbecue Sauce, sauté the chopped onion in the oil in a medium saucepan until tender. Add the ketchup, water, brown sugar, lemon juice, Worcestershire, mustard, salt and pepper sauce. Simmer, uncovered, for 15 minutes, stirring frequently.

For the Ribs, place the ribs in a 9 × 13-inch baking pan; cover with the Barbecue Sauce. Arrange the lemon slices and onion rings on top of the ribs. Cover tightly with foil. Bake for 30 minutes. Reduce the heat to 275 degrees and bake for 1 hour or until tender.

YIELD | 6 to 8 servings

Coffee Molasses Brisket Sliders

Marinate for a whole day before cooking.

1 cup bourbon

1 large onion, chopped

3 tablespoons Dijon mustard

6 garlic cloves, crushed

¼ cup molasses

¼ cup soy sauce

½ cup ketchup

¼ cup packed brown sugar

1 cup strong coffee

1 teaspoon Worcestershire sauce

Dash of hot red pepper sauce

8 to 10 pounds beef brisket

Barbecue sauce

Small rolls

Mix the bourbon, onion, Dijon mustard, garlic, molasses, soy sauce, ketchup, brown sugar, coffee, Worcestershire sauce and pepper sauce in a large resealable plastic bag.

Trim the fat from the brisket and add the brisket to the bag. Marinate in the refrigerator for 24 hours, turning the bag occasionally.

Preheat the oven to 250 degrees.

Transfer the meat and marinade to a large baking pan. Cover and cook for 4 to 5 hours or until the brisket shreds easily with a fork, basting occasionally.

Remove the brisket from the marinade and cut into thin slices. Serve with your favorite barbecue sauce and small rolls.

YIELD | 20 servings

Baked Bean Quintet

This easy and delicious recipe came from Rob, Bob's enlisted aide.

    6 slices bacon
    1 cup chopped onion,
    1 garlic clove, minced
    1 (16-ounce) can butter beans, drained
    1 (16-ounce) can lima bean, drained
    1 (16-ounce) can pork and beans
    1 (15-ounce) can red kidney beans, drained
    1 (15-ounce) can garbanzo beans, drained
    ¾ cup ketchup
    ½ cup light molasses
    ¼ cup packed brown sugar
    1 tablespoon Worcestershire sauce
    1 tablespoon prepared mustard
    ¼ teaspoon pepper
    1 onion, sliced into rings

Preheat the oven to 375 degrees.

Fry the bacon in a skillet until crisp. Drain all but 2 tablespoons of drippings in the skillet. Crumble the bacon.

Cook the onion and garlic in the drippings until the onions are tender but not brown.

Combine the bacon, onion mixture, butter beans, lima beans, pork and beans, kidney beans and garbanzo beans in a large bowl and mix well. Stir in the ketchup, molasses, brown sugar, Worcestershire sauce, mustard and pepper. Pour into a 2½-quart bean pot or baking dish. Cover and bake for 1 hour. Arrange the onion rings over the top. Bake, uncovered, for 15 minutes longer.

YIELD | **12 to 14 servings**

Deviled Eggs

A little jalapeño, cheese and onion add a little kick to the traditional stuffed egg.

    12 eggs
    4 slices bacon
    3 jalapeños
    1 cup finely shredded sharp Cheddar cheese
    ⅓ to ½ cup mayonnaise
    ¼ cup minced red onion
    2 tablespoons spicy brown mustard

GARNISH

    Paprika

Place the eggs in a large saucepan; cover with water. Bring to a boil. Remove from heat and let eggs stand in the hot water for 15 minutes. Drain; cool under cold running water. Return the eggs to the pan, put a lid on the saucepan and shake to loosen the egg shells from the eggs.

Fry the bacon in a large skillet until crisp. Drain on paper towels. Crumble the bacon.

Remove the seeds and membranes from the jalapeños. Mince 1 of the jalapeños and slice the other 2 jalapeños into 12 thin strips each.

Cut the eggs lengthwise into halves, placing the yolks in a bowl. Mash the yolks with a fork. Stir in the minced jalapeño, cheese, mayonnaise, onion and mustard. Spoon the yolk mixture into the egg halves. Sprinkle with the crumbled bacon. Garnish each half with a sprinkle of paprika and a strip of jalapeño.

YIELD | **24 servings**

WILD RICE AND KIDNEY BEAN SALAD

Broccoli Salad

A friend gave me this recipe over 20 years ago, and it is still one of my favorites!

1 cup mayonnaise
¼ cup sugar
2 tablespoons apple cider vinegar
8 cups broccoli florets
½ cup salted peanuts
½ cup chopped red onion
½ cup raisins
1 cup sliced strawberries, or 1 small can mandarin oranges, drained

Combine the mayonnaise, sugar and vinegar in a small bowl and mix well. Mix the broccoli, peanuts, onion, raisins and strawberries in a salad bowl. Stir in the desired amount of the mayonnaise mixture. Cover and refrigerate for at least 1 hour before serving.

YIELD | 8 to 10 servings

• • •

Wild Rice and Kidney Bean Salad

A new twist on a classic picnic salad.

1 (6-ounce) package long grain and wild rice mix
1 cup chicken broth
1 cup orange juice
⅓ cup water
2 (16-ounce) cans kidney beans, rinsed and drained
3 hard-boiled eggs, peeled and diced
1 large onion, minced

½ cup mayonnaise
¼ teaspoon salt
½ teaspoon pepper
⅛ teaspoon cayenne pepper
½ cup sliced almonds, toasted

GARNISH
Finely chopped fresh parsley

Cook the rice according to the package directions, using the chicken broth, orange juice and water for the liquid. Stir in the beans, eggs, onion, mayonnaise, salt, pepper and cayenne pepper. Cover and chill for 2 hours. Sprinkle with almonds just before serving. Garnish with parsley.

YIELD | 8 to 10 servings

• • •

Ice Cream Pots

An impressive ice cream dessert served in clay pots (pictured on page 99).

½ package chocolate sandwich cookies
12 (3-inch-tall) clay flowerpots with saucers
½ gallon ice cream (any flavor)
2 cups crushed Heath bars
Drinking straws, cut into 1-inch pieces

Process the cookies to coarse crumbs in a food processor.

Layer ½ to 1 inch of the cookie crumbs in the bottom of each flowerpot. Add the ice cream to within 1 inch of the top of the pots. Top with equal portions of the crushed candy. Place a straw piece upright in the center of the pot, pressing it in even with the candy. Freeze until ready to serve.

Remove from the freezer and insert a fresh flower or a sparkler in the straw piece.

YIELD | 12 ice cream pots

Crepe Luncheon

I remember when crepes were a popular party food. A crepe maker became a common wedding gift because of the popularity of crepes. Crepes are fun to make and so delicious to eat, so why not bring them back into vogue? To host a Crepe Luncheon, you can make the crepes for your guests or let them prepare their own. Crepes can be made ahead of time, which makes it a stress-free get-together. A combination of main course crepes and dessert crepes makes for a yummy luncheon.

INVITATION

A crepe-shaped invitation is easy to make. Using tan construction paper, cut out a 6-inch circle. Fold the circle in half. Write "Crepe Luncheon" on the front and then write the invitation inside.

DECORATIONS AND ACTIVITY

Set up two tables: one for luncheon crepes and another for dessert crepes. Electric crepe makers are ideal, but you can also use small skillets set up in your kitchen.

For make-your-own crepes, set up tables filled with bowls of crepe batter and filling ingredients. You may also make the crepes and fillings ahead of time and have your guests fill them with their choice of fillings. I have included 3 separate crepe batter recipes. You may use all 3 or find your favorite one to use.

★ MENU ★

Cranberry Vodka Tonic

Recipe from Michael Chiarello of Bottega. Make the cranberry and vodka mixture a week before serving.

16 ounces fresh cranberries

1 cup sugar

2 teaspoons vanilla extract, or 1 vanilla bean, split lengthwise

3 cups vodka

Ice

1 liter tonic water

GARNISH

Lime wheels

Combine the cranberries and sugar in a medium saucepan over medium heat. Add the vanilla extract or vanilla bean. Cook for 5 to 6 minutes or until the cranberries burst, stirring frequently.

Divide the vodka evenly between 2 large jars. Add equal portions of the cranberry mixture to each jar. Cover and refrigerate for 1 week.

Strain the vodka mixture into a clean jar, discarding the cranberries. Cover and store the flavored vodka in the refrigerator until serving time.

For each tonic, pour ¼ cup of the flavored vodka over ice in a tall glass; top off with tonic water. Garnish with a lime wheel.

YIELD | 16 drinks

Chicken Crepes

Bringing back an old favorite. Note that the crepe batter must rest for at least 1 hour before cooking.

CREPES

1 cup all-purpose flour

3 eggs

1½ cups milk

Dash of salt

Vegetable oil

CHICKEN FILLING

¼ cup (½ stick) unsalted butter

2 shallots, chopped

8 ounces mushrooms, thinly sliced

¼ cup all-purpose flour

2 cups chicken broth

Salt and pepper to taste

3 tablespoons dry sherry

1½ cups heavy cream

2 cups chopped cooked chicken

1 pound fresh asparagus, cut into bite-size pieces and cooked tender-crisp, or 1 (10-ounce) package frozen chopped spinach, thawed and squeezed dry

Wine and Cheese Sauce (recipe follows)

For the Crepes, combine the flour, eggs, milk and salt in a blender. Blend until smooth. Let stand for 1 to 2 hours, or refrigerate for up to 24 hours.

Brush a 6-inch skillet or crepe maker with oil, coating the bottom and sides. Heat the skillet until very hot but not smoking. Pour 2 tablespoons of the batter into the skillet, tilting to cover the bottom. Cook for 1 minute or until brown. Turn and cook about 30 seconds longer. Use immediately, or wrap in plastic wrap, refrigerate or cool, place in an airtight container and freeze.

For the Chicken Filling, melt the butter in a skillet. Add the shallots and mushrooms and sauté until tender. Add the flour and cook for 1 to 2 minutes or until well incorporated. Add the chicken broth gradually, cooking and stirring until slightly thickened. Add the sherry and cream and heat through. Add the chicken and spinach or asparagus; salt and pepper to taste. Cool slightly.

Preheat the oven to 350 degrees.

Spoon about 3 tablespoons of the chicken filling onto each crepe and roll up tightly. Place seam down in a greased baking dish. Pour the Wine and Cheese Sauce over the crepes. Bake for 5 to 10 minutes or until the sauce is bubbly. (Or cover with plastic wrap and refrigerate for 1 day or freeze for up to 3 days. Bring to room temperature before baking.)

YIELD | 12 to 14 crepes

WINE AND CHEESE SAUCE

3 tablespoons butter

3 tablespoons all-purpose flour

1 cup milk

1 cup chicken broth

½ cup heavy cream

¼ cup dry white wine

¼ cup shredded Parmesan or Gruyère cheese

Melt the butter in a medium saucepan. Add the flour, whisking to incorporate. Whisk in the milk, blending well. Add the chicken broth and cream and cook, whisking as the sauce thickens. Add the wine and continue to cook and stir until thickened. The sauce should be the consistency of heavy cream. Add the cheese and mix well.

Yield: about 3 cups

Hot Curried Fruit Compote

A recipe from my grandmother.

2 tablespoons butter, at room temperature

¼ cup packed brown sugar

1½ teaspoons curry powder

1 (16-ounce) can peach halves, drained

1 (16-ounce) can pear halves, drained

1 (16-ounce) can apricot halves, drained

1 (16-ounce) can pineapple chunks, drained

1 (16-ounce) can dark cherries or maraschino cherries, drained

¼ cup slivered almonds, toasted

Preheat the oven to 325 degrees.

Combine the butter, brown sugar and curry powder in a small bowl and mix well.

Cut the peach, pear and apricot halves into halves. Combine the peaches, pears, apricots and pineapple chunks in a roasting pan. Add the butter mixture and mix gently. Bake for 15 minutes. Add the cherries and bake for 15 minutes longer. Top with the toasted almonds. Serve warm.

YIELD | 8 to 10 servings

Blueberry Cheese Crepes

Another forgotten favorite.

CREPES

2 eggs

1 cup milk

2 tablespoons butter, melted

1 cup all-purpose flour

¼ teaspoon salt

Butter for frying

CHEESE FILLING

16 ounces cream cheese, softened

8 ounces cottage cheese

3 tablespoons confectioners' sugar

¾ teaspoon vanilla extract

BLUEBERRY SAUCE

1 to 1¼ cups blueberry pie filling

½ teaspoon grated lemon peel

Sour cream (optional)

For the Crepes, beat the eggs with an electric mixer in a bowl until foamy. Add the milk and 2 tablespoons butter and beat well. Add the flour and salt and beat until smooth.

Melt a little butter in an 8-inch skillet over medium-high heat, tilting to coat. Pour 3 tablespoons of the batter into the skillet, tilting to spread evenly. Fry for 2 minutes or until light brown on one side. Transfer the crepes browned side down to tea towels to cool.

For the Cheese Filling, combine the cream cheese, cottage cheese, confectioners' sugar and vanilla extract in a medium bowl and mix well.

Spoon ½ cup of the Cheese Filling onto the center of the browned side of each crepe; fold the sides over the filling to cover.

Melt half of the 2 tablespoons butter in a 10-inch skillet over medium heat. Add half of the crepes and fry until golden brown, turning once. Remove to a serving platter and cover to keep warm. Cook the remaining crepes in the remaining butter.

For the Blueberry Sauce, heat the pie filling and lemon peel in a small saucepan on the stove or in a small bowl in the microwave, stirring occasionally.

Serve the crepes with the Blueberry Sauce and sour cream, if desired.

YIELD | 12 crepes

Cheese Crepes

A crepe recipe from our son-in-law's brother.

CREPES

3 eggs

3 cups milk

¼ cup (½ stick) butter, melted

1½ cups all-purpose flour

2 tablespoons sugar

¼ teaspoon salt

½ teaspoon baking powder

¼ teaspoon baking soda

2 teaspoons ground cardamom

Butter for frying

CINNAMON FILLING

16 ounces cottage cheese

½ cup sugar

1 teaspoon vanilla extract

1 teaspoon ground cinnamon

Sour cream and jam

For the Crepes, beat the eggs with an electric mixer in a medium bowl until foamy. Add the milk and ¼ cup butter and beat well. Add the flour, sugar, salt, baking powder, baking soda and cardamom and beat until smooth.

Heat a little butter in an 8-inch skillet over medium-high heat, tilting to coat. Pour 3 tablespoons of the batter into the skillet, tilting to spread evenly. Fry for 2 minutes or until light brown on one side. Transfer the crepes browned side down to tea towels to cool.

For the Cinnamon Filling, stir the cottage cheese, sugar, vanilla and cinnamon together in a bowl until well blended.

Spoon 2 tablespoons of the filling onto the browned side of each crepe; fold the sides over the filling to cover. Fry the crepes in butter in a skillet over medium heat for 5 minutes or until golden brown. Serve with sour cream and jam.

YIELD | 12 crepes

TIPS

WINE STAIN | To help clean wine off a tablecloth, pour a good amount of salt, baking soda, or artificial sweetener on top of the liquid to absorb it.

Seafood Boil

A Seafood Boil is a fun and easy party. Rumor has it that a soldier was asked to feed 100 of his fellow troops. He needed something simple, using the ingredients he had on hand and so this one-pot wonder, the Seafood Boil, was born. You may also see it by other names, such as Low Country Boil, but regardless of what it is called, this one-pot meal is fabulous and EASY! It has become one of our most requested meals when friends visit us at our home in lower Alabama.

A Seafood Boil can be done inside your home or outside. I would plan to have it outside. But if the day turns rainy, you can easily move it inside and cook on your stove. Boiled down to its essence, a Seafood Boil is simply a large pot of really good seafood, sausage, corn and potatoes boiled in a fragrant Louisiana-style broth and then drained and dumped on a table covered with newspaper or brown paper, ready for your hungry crowd to dig into. It's a fun and extremely easy way to feed a large crowd. Make it even easier by using rolls of paper towels for napkins and paper or plastic plates. After the meal, the paper is rolled up, along with any food scraps, plates and paper towels, and tossed in the garbage can! How easy is that?

INVITATION

Plan ahead and visit lacrawfish.com and order crawfish bibs. They are only 15 cents each. Write the invitations on the bibs and fold them up. Place them in envelopes and send to your invitees. You can order extras to have on hand for your seafood boil, if desired.

DECORATIONS

So simple here! Set up a table outside and cover it with newspaper or brown paper. If you have some fish netting, you can drape that over the table as well. Have any seashells or decorative crabs or lobsters? Adorn your table with them. You might want to remove them before dumping the cooked food on the table, but they are nice for setting the tone for the party until then. Use rolls of paper towels in buckets or place them directly on the table to add to the simplicity of this party.

★ MENU ★

SERVE WITH | Crusty Bread and Beer

Beachcombers

A refreshing drink.

1 cup vodka

½ cup banana liqueur

½ cup pear nectar

1 tablespoon fresh lemon juice

Ice

GARNISH

Edible flowers or orange slices

Combine the vodka, liqueur, pear nectar and lemon juice in a cocktail shaker. Shake to mix. Pour into ice-filled glasses. Garnish with edible flowers or orange slices.

YIELD | 4 drinks

. . .

Crab Cakes

You will never want to try any other crab cake recipe—this is the best!

1 pound fresh jumbo lump crabmeat

1 large egg

¼ cup mayonnaise

1½ teaspoons Dijon mustard

1½ teaspoons Old Bay seasoning

1 teaspoon fresh lemon juice

½ teaspoon Worcestershire sauce

¼ teaspoon salt

1¼ cups fresh bread crumbs, preferably from Pepperidge Farm thin sandwich bread (do not use dried bread crumbs)

1 tablespoon chopped flat leaf parsley

2 tablespoons unsalted butter

1 tablespoon olive oil

Tartar Sauce (recipe follows)

Lemon wedges (optional)

Drain the crabmeat, if necessary, and sort through for shells. (Jumbo lump crabmeat normally does not have any shells.) Place the crabmeat in a bowl and set aside.

Whisk the egg, mayonnaise, Dijon mustard, Old Bay seasoning, lemon juice, Worcestershire sauce and salt in a bowl. Add the mixture to the crabmeat and mix with your hands. Do not overmix. Add the bread crumbs and parsley and mix gently. Cover with plastic wrap and refrigerate for 1 to 3 hours.

Shape the mixture into 8 cakes about 1 inch thick. Heat the butter and olive oil together in a skillet until frothy. Add the crab cakes and cook for 4 minutes or until golden brown. Turn over and cook for 4 minutes longer. Serve with Tartar Sauce and lemon wedges.

YIELD | 8 crab cakes

TARTAR SAUCE

Adjust the amount of each ingredient to suit your taste.

1 cup mayonnaise

1 to 2 whole Claussen pickles, chopped

2 tablespoons finely chopped onion

1 to 2 tablespoons pickle juice, or to taste

Garlic powder to taste

Combine the mayonnaise, pickles and onion in a small bowl and mix well. Add the pickle juice and garlic powder and mix well. Cover and refrigerate for at least 1 hour before serving.

Yield: about 1½ cups

Seafood Boil

We use a 44-quart pot with a removable basket for our Seafood Boil. You can find a variety of turkey fryer/deep fryer sets at stores such as Home Depot or Lowe's. Buying a set complete with stand and propane makes this super easy. It can also be used to fry a turkey and many other uses. I think buying the complete set is well worth the expense!

2 (3-ounce) packages classic Zatarain's dry shrimp and crab boil (not the hot variety)

½ (4-ounce) bottle liquid Zatarain's shrimp boil

6 lemons, quartered

5 garlic heads, cut horizontally into halves

1 (12-ounce) can of beer

12 new potatoes, halved

2 large onions, quartered

6 ears corn, cut into thirds

2 pounds andouille sausage, cut into 1- to 2-inch pieces

5 pounds unpeeled large shrimp

1 (2-pound) bag of clams

Fill a very large pot fitted with a strainer basket two-thirds full of water. Add the shrimp and crab boil, liquid shrimp boil, lemons, garlic and beer. Bring to a boil. Add the potatoes and onions and cook for about 10 minutes. Add the corn and sausage and cook for 10 minutes. Add the shrimp and clams and cook for 4 minutes or until the shrimp turn pink.

Lift out the basket and pour the seafood and vegetables onto a paper-covered table. Discard any clams that do not open. Serve some of the cooking liquid in a bowl for dipping.

YIELD | 10 to 12 servings

Chocolate Chiffon Pie

A yummy make-ahead frozen dessert.

1 cup (6 ounces) semisweet chocolate morsels

½ cup Choclair chocolate coconut liqueur

½ cup sugar

¼ cup water

1 egg white

1 teaspoon vanilla extract

1 teaspoon lemon juice

1¼ cups heavy whipping cream, whipped

1 (9-inch) pie shell, baked

GARNISH

2 tablespoons sliced almonds, toasted

Melt the chocolate morsels with the liqueur in a small saucepan over medium-low heat, stirring to blend; cool.

Combine the sugar, water, egg white, vanilla and lemon juice in a small mixing bowl. Beat until soft peaks form. Add half the melted chocolate and ¾ cup of the whipped cream to the egg white mixture and fold in gently.

Spoon half the egg white mixture into the baked piecrust. Drizzle with the remaining melted chocolate. Top with the remaining egg white mixture. Freeze until ready to serve.

Garnish servings with the remaining whipped cream and the toasted almonds.

YIELD | 6 to 8 servings

Wheelbarrow Brigade

Making families feel welcome to their new home is an integral component of military life. As exciting as it is to look forward to your new assignment, it is also stressful, particularly for children, as they face the prospect of making new friends and fitting into their new community. The Wheelbarrow Brigade is a great way to bring the community together in a stress-free, fun gathering. We first did this when we were stationed at Fort Riley, Kansas, in 1990. A chaplain started it, and we have taken the idea with us to every installation we have been to since then. We also started it in our civilian neighborhood after Bob retired. It is always a big success!

Wheelbarrow Brigade brings families together to meet one another and socialize, and all it takes is a wheelbarrow, some ice, and a couple of tables. Sunday afternoon from 1400 to 1600 or 1500 to 1700 works best. Most families are home at that time and not busy with family activities.

The host of the first Wheelbarrow Brigade buys a new wheelbarrow. These are available inexpensively at any home supply store. (Keep the receipt because you will find that your neighbors will not mind chipping in for the cost of the wheelbarrow since everyone is going to benefit from it.)

The event is held in someone's front yard or in an open area in the neighborhood. On the day of the event, it is the host's responsibility to fill the wheelbarrow with ice. You'll need a small table for blank nametags, markers, and a sign-in sheet for people to fill out so you will have a roster for the future. You will also need a table for the snacks, paper plates, and napkins. A trash can is set out, as well.

As neighbors arrive, they put their drinks on ice in the wheelbarrow and their snacks on the table. They set up their chairs, fill out a nametag and sign in. How easy is that? The children run off to play and the adults mingle. When the event is over, everyone takes their chairs and remaining snacks and drinks home, and there is nothing left to clean up. Voila!

A day or two after the event, the host wheels the wheelbarrow to someone else's yard, signifying they are the next host. The new host decides on a date for the next Wheelbarrow Brigade, sends out the flyers and the process starts again.

We have found that doing it every other week in the summer works well. When school starts, we normally go down to once a month. When cold weather hits, the wheelbarrow is stored until spring.

★ MENU ★

INVITATION

At least a week before the event, pass out flyers announcing the Wheelbarrow Brigade (sample wording is included below). Kids love this chore! Don't ask for RSVPs—you don't need a head count. Remember, the purpose of the Wheelbarrow Brigade is to have an easy, stress-free get-together for everyone.

Here's an example of the Wheelbarrow Brigade invitation that was sent out while we were at Fort Riley. Change the wording to suit your neighborhood.

Wheelbarrow Brigade

It has come to the attention of several residents of Barry, Forsyth, Sheridan, Schofield and Pershing Avenues that folk don't get together and visit the way they used to. In an effort to remedy this sad situation, we shall institute the Wheelbarrow Brigade. Our first muster will be at 1500 hours, August 1, at Bob and Lynn Wilson's, 23B Sheridan Avenue. At that time we will make a roster of Wheelbarrow Brigade members. If you are unable to make the muster, give Bob or Lynn a call and they will add you to the roster. Or better yet, come to the next muster and add your name.

Rules for the Wheelbarrow Brigade will be as follows:

1. *The wheelbarrow will be delivered to a new host no later than 7 days after the previous Wheelbarrow Brigade.*

2. *It is the responsibility of the new host to distribute flyers for the next muster, to be held within 14 days of the previous muster.*

3. *The day of the muster, the host is to fill the wheelbarrow with one case of beer, ice, plus chips and dip for snacking.*

4. *Other members of the Wheelbarrow Brigade attending shall bring to the muster:*

    A) *six-pack of beer OR*

    B) *a six-pack of soft drinks OR*

    C) *a bottle of wine AND*

    D) *lawn chairs*

5. *Snacks shall be provided by guests with the following restrictions: All snacks must come directly from a box, bag or deli. This is an extremely casual get-together and little or no advance preparation is warranted or desired.*

6. *The wheelbarrow must pass through all members once before it can return to a house that it has already visited.*

7. *New residents of the community will be invited once to see if they would like to join the Wheelbarrow Brigade. If they choose (we hope), their name will be put on the roster and they will immediately become eligible to host the Wheelbarrow Brigade.*

The purpose of the Wheelbarrow Brigade is to have time to sit, relax, chat, visit, and build lasting friendships. If all that appeals to you, please join us! This is for the entire family!

MENU

Wheelbarrow Brigade is entirely about bringing a snack from a box or bag, but here are some appetizers if you decide to offer a homemade snack.

Long Island Iced Tea

A refreshing and potent drink.

Ice
1 ounce vodka
1 ounce gold tequila
1 ounce light rum
1 ounce gin
1 ounce Cointreau or triple sec
5 ounces sweet-and-sour mix
2 ounces cola

GARNISH
1 lime wedge

Fill a cocktail shaker with ice; add the vodka, tequila, rum, gin, Cointreau and sweet-and-sour mix. Cover and shake until the shaker is frosty.

Place a couple of ice cubes in a highball glass and strain the drink into the glass. Top off with cola. Garnish with a lime wedge.

YIELD | 1 iced tea

• • •

Fiesta Dip

A tried-and-true recipe that can be made a day ahead.

2 to 3 avocados, mashed
2 tablespoons lemon juice
½ teaspoon salt
¼ teaspoon pepper
1 cup sour cream
½ cup mayonnaise
1 package taco seasoning mix
3 tomatoes, chopped
1 bunch green onions including green tops, chopped
1 (2- to 3-ounce) can sliced black olives, drained
2 (10-ounce) cans bean dip
8 ounces Cheddar cheese, shredded
Tortilla chips or scoop-shaped corn chips

Stir together the avocados, lemon juice, salt and pepper in a small bowl. Combine the sour cream, mayonnaise and taco seasoning mix in second bowl. Toss the tomatoes, green onions and olives together in a third bowl.

To serve, spread the bean dip on a platter. Layer with the avocado mixture, sour cream mixture and tomato mixture in the order given. Sprinkle cheese on top. Refrigerate until serving time. Serve with tortilla chips or scoop-shaped corn chips.

YIELD | 8 to 10 servings

• • •

Caramel Apple

Who doesn't love a caramel apple?

1 (8-ounce) block cream cheese
1 (8-ounce) jar caramel sauce
2 to 3 Heath bars, crushed
4 to 5 green apples, sliced

Place the cream cheese on a plate. Top with the caramel sauce and sprinkle with the crushed candy. Arrange the apple slices around the cream cheese. Provide a spreader for guests to use.

YIELD | 12 to 15 servings

Lower Alabama Caviar

A great summer appetizer.

¾ cup balsamic vinegar

½ cup extra-virgin olive oil

¼ cup sugar

2 teaspoons salt

1 teaspoon black pepper

2 (15-ounce) cans black-eyed peas, rinsed and drained

2 (15-ounce) cans black beans, rinsed and drained

1 cup chopped red onion

1½ cups quartered cherry tomatoes

1 or 2 avocados, diced

Fresh cilantro to taste

Tortilla chips

Combine the vinegar, olive oil, sugar, salt and pepper in a jar and shake until well blended.

Combine the black-eyed peas, black beans, onion and tomatoes in a large bowl and mix well. Stir in the avocadoes and cilantro gently. Add desired amount of dressing and mix well. Cover and refrigerate for at least 2 hours. Serve with tortilla chips.

YIELD | 20 to 24 servings

Tortilla Roll-Ups

My favorite tortilla roll-up recipe. Make ahead and slice right before serving.

8 ounces sour cream

8 ounces cream cheese, softened

1 (4-ounce) can chopped green chilies, drained

1 (4-ounce) can chopped black olives

1 cup grated Cheddar cheese

½ cup finely chopped green onions

Garlic powder to taste

Salt to taste

5 (10-inch) flour tortillas

Salsa

GARNISH

Diced red and yellow bell peppers

Mix the sour cream, cream cheese, chilies, olives, Cheddar cheese and onions. Season with garlic powder and salt. Spread a layer of the mixture over each tortilla. Roll up the tortillas and wrap tightly with plastic wrap, making sure the rolls-ups are sealed well. Refrigerate for several hours to chill.

Unwrap the roll-ups and cut into ½- to ¾-inch slices. Spoon salsa into a small dish. Place the dish in the middle of a serving platter and arrange the roll-ups around the salsa.

YIELD | 30 to 36 roll-ups

 TIPS

SWEET CORN | When boiling corn on the cob, add a pinch of sugar to help bring out the corn's natural sweetness.

Fiesta Olé!

A Mexican party is fun and easy to give because you can prepare so many of the dishes ahead of time, giving you time to truly enjoy your evening. Set the tone by hand-delivering invitations tied to personalized margarita glasses.

As your guests arrive with their personalized glass, the margaritas are ready for pouring. Additional glasses are set out so that everyone can enjoy a "welcome margarita." Appetizers can be placed around the room on brightly colored dishes. Festive Mexican music in the background is a must.

INVITATION

Buy inexpensive margarita glasses. Write each couple's last name on the base of a glass using a glass-writing pen (these can be found at hobby stores). Tie an invitation to the stem using raffia. Hand-deliver one glass per couple with instructions that it is their entry ticket.

DECORATIONS

Bright and colorful is the theme here! Sombreros, maracas and piñatas are traditional, and there is nothing wrong with being traditional with your Fiesta Olé! Festive Mexican music continues the party theme.

Make your own mini piñatas as decorations that guests can take as they leave. Blow up 6-inch balloons; tie a string on the end for hanging the balloons. Cut newspaper into 1 × 6-inch strips. Make paper mâché paste by combining 2 parts flour to 1 part water in a large bowl. Dip the paper strips in the mixture, coating them well. Cover the balloons completely with at least three layers of strips. Hang the balloons by their strings until the paper mâché dries. After the strips dry, carefully cut out a small flap in each piñata, large enough to put candy inside the piñatas. Pull out the popped balloons. Cut colorful tissue paper cut into strips, then cut "fringe" on each strip. Cover them with the tissue paper. Fill the piñatas with candy and secure the flaps with tape. Hang these around the house as decorations and let each couple take one home as a gift.

★ MENU ★

ACTIVITY

Want to play some games? I found these game ideas on PartyGamesPlus.com:

Sombrero Hat Game

Participants stand in a circle with a sombrero on one person's head. Start the music, and the sombrero is passed from head to head. The person who has the sombrero on his/her head when the music stops is eliminated. Keep playing until everyone except the winner is eliminated.

Hot Chili Pepper Eating Contest

Who is crazy enough to want to be part of a hot pepper eating contest? We guarantee some of your guests will!

Taco Battle

This is a game best played outside. Each couple stands a few feet apart facing each other. (If you really want competition, they should stand several yards apart.) One spouse holds a crisp taco shell on a wooden spoon, runs to his/her spouse and slides the taco shell off the spoon into a bowl. The spouse must place the taco shell on his/her own spoon and run to the other end and deposit his/her shell in the bowl. The couple that does it the quickest without breaking the shell wins.

MENU

I have so many fiesta recipes and am including all of my favorites. Choose what best suits your party.

 TIPS

RIPEN AVOCADOS | To ripen a hard avocado more quickly, place in a brown bag, and let stand for 1 to 2 days.

Kathy's Margaritas

These are the best margaritas ever!

1½ parts tequila

1 part triple sec

1 part Rose's lime juice

Ice

Margarita salt

GARNISH

Grand Marnier

Combine the tequila, triple sec and lime juice in a cocktail shaker. Fill the shaker with ice and shake until the shaker is frosty. Strain into salt-rimmed margarita glasses. Garnish with a drizzle of Grand Marnier.

YIELD | 1 margarita

PITCHER OF KATHY'S MARGARITAS

1½ cups tequila

1 cup triple sec

1 cup Rose's lime juice

Ice

Margarita salt

GARNISH: Grand Marnier

Mix the tequila, triple sec and lime juice in a pitcher. Pour 2 cups of the mixture into a cocktail shaker, fill with ice and shake until the shaker is frosty. Pour into salt-rimmed margarita glasses. Garnish with a drizzle of Grand Marnier.

Yield: 6 margaritas

Guacamole

4 medium or large avocados, cut into ¼-inch pieces

2 medium or large tomatoes, cut into ¼-inch pieces

4 green onions, finely chopped

¼ to ½ cup finely chopped fresh cilantro

2 tablespoons fresh lime juice

1 medium garlic clove, minced

1 to 2 teaspoons salt, or to taste

1 fresh jalapeño, chopped (optional)

Combine the avocados, tomatoes, green onions, cilantro, lime juice, garlic, salt and jalapeño in a serving bowl and mix gently. Cover with plastic wrap, pressing it directly onto the surface to prevent discoloration. Refrigerate for 1 hour.

YIELD | 4 to 5 cups

Mexican Hot Layered Dip

This is one of my most frequently requested recipes, and it is so easy to make!

1 pound ground beef

1 medium onion, chopped

Salt and pepper to taste

1 (16-ounce) can refried beans

1 (4-ounce) can chopped green chilies

1 to 1½ cups mixed shredded Monterey Jack and Cheddar cheese

¾ cup prepared taco sauce

2 avocados, pitted and chopped

1 teaspoon lemon juice

¼ cup chopped green onions

½ cup black olives, sliced

1 cup sour cream

1 to 1½ cups mixed shredded Monterey Jack and Cheddar cheese

¼ cup chopped green onions

Tortilla chips or scoop-shaped corn chips

Brown the ground beef with the onion in a skillet over medium heat, stirring to crumble; drain. Season with salt and pepper.

Spread the refried beans in a shallow 9 × 13-inch baking dish; top with the ground beef mixture. Layer with the green chilies and 1 to 1½ cups cheese. Drizzle the taco sauce over the cheese. Cover and refrigerate if making ahead of time.

Preheat the oven to 375 degrees. Bake the dip, uncovered, for 20 to 25 minutes or until bubbly.

Toss the avocados with the lemon juice in a small bowl. Spread over the layers. Sprinkle the olives over the avocado mixture. Spread the sour cream on top and sprinkle with 1 to 1½ cups cheese and ¼ cup green onions. Serve immediately with tortilla chips or corn chips.

YIELD | 10 to 12 servings

Note

You can substitute 16 ounces guacamole for the avocados and lemon juice.

. . .

Bacon-Wrapped Jalapeños

These have a mild taste so all your guests can enjoy them.

12 jalapeños

4 ounces cream cheese, softened

½ cup shredded sharp Cheddar cheese, or cheese of choice

12 slices bacon

Preheat the oven to 400 degrees. Line a baking sheet with aluminum foil.

Cut the jalapeños lengthwise into halves without cutting all the way through. Open the jalapeños like a book. Remove the seeds and membranes carefully.

Combine the cream cheese and Cheddar cheese in a bowl and mix well. Fill each jalapeño with cheese mixture, closing the jalapeño around the filling and wrapping with a bacon slice. Arrange on the prepared pan. Bake for 15 minutes or until the bacon is crispy. Serve hot.

YIELD | 12 jalapeños

Taco Soup

An easy and good-tasting recipe from my daughter's mother-in-law.

1 pound ground beef

1 onion, chopped

1 package taco seasoning mix

2 (15-ounce) cans red kidney beans

2 (28-ounce) cans diced tomatoes

Corn chips, sour cream, guacamole and shredded cheese

Brown the ground beef with the onion in a Dutch oven, stirring to crumble the ground beef; drain.

Stir in the taco seasoning mix, beans and tomatoes and simmer for 20 minutes.

Serve with corn chips, sour cream, guacamole and cheese.

YIELD | 4 to 6 servings

• • •

Chiles Rellenos

A recipe from a dear friend born in California— she knows her Mexican food!

CHILES

7 ounces canned whole California green chilies, drained

1 (8-ounce) block Monterey Jack cheese, cut into ½ × 3-inch strips

1 to 1½ cups all-purpose flour

3 eggs, separated

1 tablespoon water

3 tablespoons all-purpose flour

¼ teaspoon salt

Vegetable oil for frying

Salt to taste

TOPPINGS

¼ cup chopped onion

1 tablespoon vegetable oil

½ cup Snap-E Tom tomato and chile cocktail juice

¼ cup salsa

1 cup shredded Cheddar cheese

GARNISH

4 green onion tops, sliced

Rinse the chilies and cut a slit down the side of each chili. Remove the seeds and membranes carefully. Stuff each chili with a cheese strip, slightly overlapping the cut edges of the chili to enclose the cheese.

Spread 1 to 1½ cups flour in a shallow pan. Roll each chili in the flour to coat. Gently shake off the excess flour. Place on a plate.

Beat the egg whites in a bowl until soft peaks form. Beat the egg yolks with the water, 3 tablespoons flour and the salt in another bowl until thick and creamy. Fold the egg yolk mixture gently into the egg whites.

Heat 1 to 2 inches of oil in a wide frying pan over medium heat. Dip the stuffed chilies into the batter, place on a saucer and slide the chilies carefully into the hot oil. Cook for 3 to 4 minutes per side or until golden brown. Drain on paper towels.

Sauté the onion in 1 tablesoon oil until tender. Add the tomato juice and salsa and heat through.

Preheat the oven to 350 degrees.

Arrange the chilies on an ovenproof serving platter and top with the salsa mixture. Sprinkle with the shredded Cheddar cheese. Bake until the cheese is melted. Garnish with the green onions. Serve warm.

YIELD | about 8 servings

Beef Enchiladas

Can be prepared ahead of time and heated just before serving.

1½ pounds ground round
1 medium onion, chopped
1 (16-ounce) can refried beans
1 teaspoon salt
⅛ teaspoon garlic powder
⅓ cup taco sauce
1 (3-ounce) can sliced black olives
2 (10-ounce) cans enchilada sauce
Vegetable oil for frying
12 corn tortillas
3 cups shredded Cheddar cheese

GARNISH
Sliced black olives, sour cream and hot green chili salsa

Brown the ground beef with the onion in a large skillet, stirring to crumble the ground beef; drain. Stir in the refried beans, salt, garlic powder, taco sauce and olives. Cook until bubbly.

Heat the enchilada sauce in a small saucepan. Pour half the enchilada sauce into a shallow 3-quart baking dish.

Heat about ½ inch of oil in a small skillet. Dip the tortillas, 1 at a time, into the oil to soften. Drain immediately on paper towels.

Spoon ⅓ cup of the ground beef mixture onto each tortilla and roll up. Place side by side in the baking dish. Pour the remaining enchilada sauce over the enchiladas. Top with the cheese. The enchiladas may be prepared to this point and refrigerated, covered, until ready to bake.

Preheat the oven to 350 degrees. Bake the enchiladas, uncovered, for 15 to 20 minutes or until bubbly. Garnish with black olives, sour cream and green salsa.

YIELD | 12 enchiladas

Chicken Fajitas

A simple last-minute meal.

½ cup soy sauce
½ cup sugar
¼ teaspoon garlic powder
⅛ teaspoon ground ginger
⅛ teaspoon onion powder
Salt to taste
1½ pounds chicken tenders, or boneless skinless chicken breast halves, cut into strips
1 red bell pepper, cut into strips
1 yellow bell pepper, cut into strips
1 green bell pepper, cut into strips
1 large onion, sliced
¼ cup (½ stick) butter
12 flour tortillas

GARNISH
Chopped green onions, salsa, sour cream, cilantro and shredded Cheddar cheese

Combine the soy sauce, sugar, garlic powder, ginger, onion powder and salt in a large saucepan. Bring to boil over medium heat. Add the chicken. Reduce the heat to low and simmer for 30 to 45 minutes.

Sauté the bell peppers and onion in the butter in a skillet until tender-crisp.

Wrap the tortillas in foil and heat in a 350-degree oven for 5 minutes, or wrap in paper towels and microwave for 30 to 60 seconds.

Drain the chicken and spoon into a bowl or onto a platter. Spoon the bell pepper mixture into a separate bowl. Place the warm tortillas next to the chicken. Allow guests to build their own fajitas, adding desired garnishes.

YIELD | 6 servings

Fried Ice Cream

Make these ahead of time, including the frying, and store in the freezer.

½ gallon vanilla ice cream

3 cups crushed cornflakes

2 teaspoons ground cinnamon

Vegetable oil for frying

GARNISH

Honey, whipped cream and chocolate
  sauce

Scoop the ice cream into 9 balls. Freeze for at least 4 hours or until frozen solid.

Combine the cornflakes and cinnamon in a shallow dish. Roll the ice cream balls in the cornflake mixture and return to the freezer for at least 4 hours.

Heat 4 to 5 inches of oil to 375 degrees in a heavy saucepan. Fry 1 ice cream ball at a time in the oil and for about 20 seconds. Garnish with honey, whipped cream and chocolate sauce.

YIELD | 9 servings

Pan of "Fried" Ice Cream

Rather than making individual servings of fried ice cream, you can make a whole pan.

½ cup (1 stick) butter

1 cup sugar

3 cups crushed cornflakes

½ gallon vanilla ice cream

¾ teaspoon cinnamon

2 tablespoons honey

GARNISH

Chocolate sauce

Whipped cream

Melt the butter in a large skillet over low heat. Add the sugar and cook until the sugar is dissolved, stirring constantly. Add the cornflakes and cook for 5 minutes or until caramelized, stirring constantly and watching carefully so the mixture does not burn.

Butter a 9 × 13-inch freezer-safe pan. Sprinkle half the cornflake mixture over the bottom of the pan. Soften the ice cream enough to mix in the cinnamon. Spread the ice cream over the cornflake layer. Top with the remaining cornflake mixture and drizzle with the honey. Freeze until firm. Garnish servings with chocolate sauce and whipped cream.

YIELD | 10 to 12 servings

Cook the Book

Book clubs have always been a favorite get-together for friends. Put a new spin on it by hosting a Cook the Book party. Choose a book that you like and ask your guests to read it before the party.

I chose *Eat, Pray, Love* for my party because I think it is a beautifully written and heartfelt memoir by author Elizabeth Gilbert. She recounts her travels to Italy, India, and Bali, which gave me three cuisines to choose from. I decided to concentrate on Italy because I love Italian food. Whether you choose *Eat, Pray, Love* or another book, develop your menu around the setting of the book. It is simple and fun to do!

Before your party, go online and download questions for your book club. You can find book club questions for almost all top-selling books.

★ MENU ★

INVITATION

Photocopy the cover of *Eat, Pray, Love*, reducing it and orienting it so the image covers half the page. Fold the page in half so it opens like a card. Write your invitation inside the "card" and mail it to your invitees.

ACTIVITY

As guests arrive, give them a glass of wine and appetizers of Fried Mozzarella, Prosciutto-Wrapped Melon, and Prosciutto-Wrapped Shrimp. Find a comfortable sitting area and discuss the book while sipping your sangria and enjoying the appetizers. Follow your discussion with a wonderful Italian dinner.

DECORATIONS

Decorating can be done around the theme of your menu or choose "book club" as the theme.

I chose an Italian theme for decorating. Red, white, and green, the colors of the Italian flag, were the colors for my party. For a centerpiece, buy large cardboard letters from a craft store (they're about a dollar each). Get the letters for ITALY and paint the IT green, the A white, and the LY red. Or you could make the T half green and half red and the L half white and half red. When placed together they look like the Italian flag. Use red and white gingham for your tablecloths.

Thin red, green, and white ribbons can be tied together around your napkins to serve as napkin rings. Add tall glass vases filled with multicolored dry pasta and tall spaghetti and/or tall thin breadsticks. Chianti wine comes in great-looking bottles; use them as part of your decorating. Put some multicolored candles in empty wine bottles and drip the wax down the side of the bottles. You can also scatter grape clusters around the tables.

Sangria

1 lemon, cut into ½-inch wheels

1 lime, cut into ½-inch wheels

2 oranges, cut into ½-inch wheels

½ cup sugar

8 ounces triple sec, chilled

8 ounces brandy, chilled

8 ounces fresh orange juice, chilled

1 (750-milliliter) bottle dry red wine,
    chilled

Place the lemon, lime and oranges in a pitcher. Sprinkle sugar over the fruit and muddle the fruit to extract some of the juices. Add the triple sec and brandy and stir well to dissolve the sugar. Stir in the orange juice and wine.

YIELD | 6 to 8 servings

. . .

Fried Mozzarella

Olive oil for frying

3 eggs

½ teaspoon salt

1½ pounds mozzarella cheese,
    cut into ½ × 2-inch strips

1 cup all-purpose flour

1 teaspoon dried Italian seasoning

1½ cups bread crumbs

1 cup grated Parmesan cheese

1 small jar marinara sauce

Heat 3 inches of olive oil in a large saucepan.

Beat the eggs with the salt in a bowl. Combine the flour and Italian seasoning in a resealable plastic bag. Add the mozzarella strips to the bag and shake to coat. Dip each strip into the eggs and coat with the bread crumbs.

Lower a few at a time into the hot olive oil. Fry until golden brown. Drain on paper towels. Serve with the marinara sauce.

YIELD | 8 servings

Prosciutto-Wrapped Melon

A refreshing appetizer!

1 cantaloupe or honeydew melon,
    cut into thin wedges

Juice of ½ lime

15 to 20 slices prosciutto

2 to 3 tablespoons good-quality balsamic
    vinegar

GARNISH

15 to 20 fresh mint leaves

Drizzle the cantaloupe with the lime juice. Wrap each wedge with a prosciutto slice. Arrange the wedges on a serving platter and drizzle with the balsamic vinegar. Garnish each wedge with a mint leaf.

YIELD | 15 to 20 servings

Prosciutto-Wrapped Shrimp

A delicious appetizer that we serve year-round.

8 (6-inch) wooden skewers

½ cup olive oil

¼ cup dry vermouth

2 teaspoons dried oregano

1 teaspoon freshly ground pepper

6 garlic cloves, crushed

16 fresh jumbo shrimp, or thawed frozen
   shrimp

16 thin slices prosciutto

Soak the wooden skewers in water for 30 minutes.

Combine the olive oil, vermouth, oregano, pepper and garlic in a resealable plastic bag. Add the shrimp and marinate in the refrigerator for 1 hour, turning once. Remove the shrimp from the marinade and wrap each with prosciutto. Thread 2 wrapped shrimp onto each wooden skewer. Broil or grill for 4 to 5 minutes or until the shrimp are cooked.

YIELD | 8 servings

TIPS

NICKED FINGER | Nicked your finger cutting vegetables? Sprinkle the cut with black pepper. It will stop the bleeding.

Eggplant Casserole

So good, even people who don't like eggplant will love this dish!

3 medium eggplants, peeled and cut into
   ¼- to ½-inch slices

2 teaspoons salt

1 cup all-purpose flour

¼ to ½ cup olive oil

1 (24-ounce) jar marinara sauce

8 ounces mozzarella cheese, thinly sliced

½ cup shredded Parmesan cheese

Preheat the oven to 400 degrees.

Sprinkle both sides of the eggplant slices with the salt. Arrange the eggplant in a single layer on paper towels. Top with another layer of paper towels and let the eggplant sweat for 20 to 25 minutes. Pat dry.

Dip the eggplant in the flour and shake off the excess. Heat ¼ cup olive oil in a large heavy skillet over medium-high heat. Brown the eggplant on both sides, adding more oil as needed. Drain on paper towels.

Pour ½ cup marinara sauce over the bottom of a lightly greased 9-inch baking dish. Layer the eggplant, marinara sauce and mozzarella cheese in the baking dish. Repeat layers and top with the Parmesan cheese. Cover and bake for 20 minutes. Uncover and bake for 10 minutes longer.

YIELD | 4 to 6 servings

Chicken Milano

A friend gave me this recipe over 20 years ago, and it continues to be an easy family favorite.

1 medium onion, chopped

1 tablespoon butter or margarine

3 cups chopped cooked chicken

1 (10-ounce) can cream of chicken soup

8 ounces sour cream

1 (4-ounce) can chopped green chilies, drained

½ cup sliced almonds

½ teaspoon oregano

¼ teaspoon salt

⅛ teaspoon pepper

10 (7-inch) flour tortillas

1 (10-ounce) can cream of chicken soup

1 cup shredded Cheddar cheese

⅓ cup milk

Preheat the oven to 350 degrees.

Sauté the onion in the butter in a large saucepan over medium heat until tender. Add the chicken, 1 can of soup, sour cream, green chilies, almonds, oregano, salt and pepper and mix well. Spoon about ½ cup of the chicken mixture onto the center of each tortilla. Roll to enclose the filling and arrange seam down in a lightly greased 9 × 13-inch baking dish.

Combine 1 can of soup, cheese and milk in a small bowl and mix well. Spoon over the tortillas. Bake, uncovered, for 35 minutes or until brown and bubbly.

YIELD | 10 servings

Note

To make the recipe even easier, buy a rotisserie chicken instead of cooking the chicken.

Spinach Cheese Manicotti

This recipe won our family's "manicotti cook-off."

8 ounces manicotti noodles

2 cups cream-style cottage cheese or ricotta cheese

1 (8-ounce) block mozzarella cheese, finely diced

⅓ cup grated Parmesan cheese

3 eggs, lightly beaten

½ teaspoon salt

⅛ teaspoon pepper

¼ teaspoon nutmeg

2 tablespoons butter or margarine, melted

1 (10-ounce) package frozen chopped spinach, thawed and squeezed dry

Tomato Herb Pasta Sauce (recipe follows)

⅓ cup grated Parmesan cheese

Preheat the oven to 350 degrees.

Cook the manicotti according to the package directions; drain.

Combine the cottage cheese, mozzarella, ⅓ cup Parmesan cheese, eggs, salt, pepper, nutmeg, butter and spinach and mix well. Pour a thin layer of the tomato sauce over the bottom of a lightly greased 9 × 13-inch baking dish.

Spoon some of the spinach mixture into each manicotti and arrange in a single layer in the baking dish. Pour the remaining sauce over the manicotti and sprinkle with ⅓ cup Parmesan cheese. Bake for 30 to 35 minutes or until bubbly.

YIELD | 6 to 8 servings

TOMATO HERB PASTA SAUCE

¼ cup (½ stick) butter or margarine

2 garlic cloves, minced

1 medium onion, chopped

1 teaspoon dried oregano

1 teaspoon dried basil

1 teaspoon dried thyme

Pinch of rubbed sage

1 (28-ounce) can Italian plum
    tomatoes, chopped

2 (15-ounce) cans tomato sauce

1 (6-ounce) can tomato paste

1 teaspoon salt

⅛ teaspoon pepper

1 teaspoon sugar

1 teaspoon red pepper flakes

Red wine (optional)

Melt the butter in a large saucepan over medium heat. Add the garlic, onion, oregano, basil, thyme and sage and cook until the onion and garlic are lightly browned. Add the tomatoes, tomato sauce, tomato paste, salt, pepper, sugar and red pepper flakes. Cover and simmer over low heat for 1 hour, adding a little red wine if the sauce becomes too thick.

Yield: 1½ quarts

Caesar Salad

A great Caesar salad.

CROUTONS

3 cups cubed country bread

3 tablespoons olive oil

½ teaspoon salt

Freshly ground black pepper to taste

SALAD

3 garlic cloves

3 anchovies

½ teaspoon kosher salt

Dash of pepper to taste

1 tablespoon Dijon mustard

Juice of ½ lemon, or to taste

1 teaspoon Worcestershire sauce

3 tablespoons olive oil

1 or 2 avocados, cut into cubes

3 romaine lettuce hearts, chopped

Shredded Parmesan cheese to taste

For the Croutons, preheat the oven to 375 degrees.

Toss the bread with the olive oil on a baking sheet. Season with the salt and pepper. Bake for 10 to 15 minutes or until golden brown, tossing occasionally. (Croutons can be made in advance and stored in an airtight container.)

For the Salad, Mash the garlic and anchovies together in a large wooden bowl. Mix in the salt, pepper and Dijon mustard. Add the lemon juice, Worcestershire sauce and olive oil and mix well. Add the avocados and toss to coat. Add the lettuce and toss to coat. Add the Croutons and Parmesan cheese just before serving.

YIELD | 8 servings

Spumoni

A refreshing dessert after a heavy Italian dinner. Choose any two flavors of ice cream you like if you do not want use the ones in the recipe.

1 tablespoon rum

1 pint French vanilla ice cream, softened

½ cup heavy whipping cream

¼ cup powdered chocolate drink mix

1 pint pistachio ice cream

Chocolate sauce, or Kahlúa Chocolate Sauce (page 177)

Freeze a 9 × 12-inch pan for 1 hour. Line the bottom and sides of the chilled pan with plastic wrap.

Stir the rum into the vanilla ice cream. Spread the ice cream over the bottom of the prepared pan. Freeze until firm.

Combine the cream and chocolate drink mix in a bowl and whip with an electric mixer until stiff peaks form. Spread over the ice cream layer. Freeze until firm.

Soften the pistachio ice cream and spread over the chocolate layer. Freeze until firm.

Remove the pan from the freezer 10 to 20 minutes before serving. Invert the pan onto a serving platter and rub the sides with a towel dampened with warm water to loosen the ice cream from the pan. Remove the pan and peel off the plastic wrap. Serve with chocolate sauce or Kahlúa Chocolate Sauce.

YIELD | 12 servings

AMAZING CLEANER | Alka-Seltzer tablets have many uses. Put 2 tablets in a glass of water to clean jewelry. Put a tablet in a vase to remove stains. To clean a thermos, fill it with water, drop in 4 tablets, and let it sit for an hour. Unclog a drain by dropping in 3 tablets followed by a cup of white vinegar. Wait a few minutes and then run the hot water to clear the drain.

Sock Hop

Even people who don't like to dance can't help but tap their feet and move a little when they hear rock-and-roll music. Reliving the '50s and '60s is just downright fun! Set the stage with an invitation written on a sock. Wearing '50s or '60s garb can be optional, but offering a prize for the "Best Dressed" increases your guests' enthusiasm to dress the part!

Also, did you know that the first TV dinner was introduced in 1953? As children, we were always excited when our parents planned an evening out because we got to go to the store and pick out our favorite TV dinner. Relive those days by making TV dinners for your guests. Order aluminum foil trays with compartments and foil lids from **kitchendance.com** or another website, or make your own trays from round or square aluminum pans, making dividers with aluminum foil. Make your TV dinners in advance and freeze them.

★ MENU ★

INVITATION

Write your invitation on a sock or tuck an invitation inside a sock. Put the sock in an envelope or tube for mailing.

DECORATIONS

Poodle skirts and t-shirts with combs rolled up in the sleeves! Use black paint or shoe polish to paint the middle of an old pair of white sneakers to resemble saddle oxfords. Old 45 records and movie posters from the period complete the décor.

ACTIVITY

Name that Tune!

Download music from the various decades and create a playlist of "snippets" of different songs. Let your guests (as couples) choose which decade they want. You will need a stopwatch or timer. Start the music and give each couple 2 minutes to name as many tunes as they can. Give a prize to the couple that names the most tunes. Be ready with a tie-breaking round.

Hula Hoop contest

I don't know about you, but I used to be a great "hula hooper." I can't do it to save my life today, but there are some people who can, so hold a hula hoop contest. Gather hula hoops and see who can hula hoop the longest.

Bubble gum blowing contest

In the movie "Grease," everyone was always chewing gum. Bring back the era by providing a piece of Bazooka bubble gum to those interested in showing their bubble gum blowing skill. See who can blow the largest bubble.

Dance

It goes without saying that you must have a dance area so you can play your favorite rock-and-roll music and relive The Twist, The Pony, and all the other favorites.

Spiked Chocolate Milkshakes

An adult milkshake.

1½ cups chocolate ice cream

½ cup milk

2 ounces bourbon

1 tablespoon Kahlúa

GARNISH

Whipped cream

Stem-on maraschino cherries

Purée the ice cream, milk, bourbon and Kahlúa in a blender until smooth. Divide between two glasses. Garnish each milkshake with whipped cream and a maraschino cherry.

YIELD | 2 milkshakes

• • •

Spiked Creamsicle Milkshakes

1 pint vanilla ice cream

3 tablespoons orange juice

3 tablespoons vodka

3 tablespoons triple sec

GARNISH

Stem-on maraschino cherries

Purée the ice cream, orange juice, vodka and triple sec in a blender until smooth. Divide between two glasses. Garnish each milkshake with a maraschino cherry.

YIELD | 2 milkshakes

Clam Dip

There are many versions of this mid-century favorite, but this is my favorite.

8 ounces cream cheese, softened

1 cup sour cream

1½ teaspoons Worcestershire sauce

2 teaspoons lemon juice

¼ teaspoon garlic salt

2 (8-ounce) cans clams

Salt and pepper to taste

Dash of hot red pepper sauce

Potato chips or raw vegetables

Beat the cream cheese with an electric mixer in a bowl until smooth. Add the sour cream, Worcestershire sauce, lemon juice and garlic salt and mix well.

Drain the clams, reserving the juice. Fold the clams gently into the cream cheese mixture. Add enough of the reserved clam juice to make of the desired consistency. Season with salt, pepper and hot sauce. Serve with potato chips or raw vegetables.

YIELD | about 24 servings

Sour Cream and Onion Dip

This dip was very popular in the 1950s and 1960s.

16 ounces sour cream

½ cup mayonnaise

1 envelope onion soup mix

Potato chips or raw vegetables

Combine the sour cream, mayonnaise and onion soup mix in a medium bowl and mix well. Serve with potato chips or raw vegetables.

YIELD | about 12 servings

• • •

Bacon-Wrapped Water Chestnuts

A delicious appetizer that can be assembled ahead of time and heated just before serving.

1 cup soy sauce

1 cup brown sugar

½ cup ketchup

2 (8-ounce) cans whole water chestnuts, drained

1 pound bacon, cut into thirds

Preheat the oven to 400 degrees.

Combine the soy sauce, brown sugar, ketchup and Worcestershire sauce in a bowl and mix well. Wrap each water chestnut with a piece of bacon and secure with a toothpick. Place wrapped water chestnuts in a 9 × 13-inch baking dish. Pour the sauce over the water chestnuts and bake for 30 minutes or until the bacon is crisp.

YIELD | about 12 servings

• • •

Tuna Tetrazzini

This retro favorite is spooned into the larger section of the TV dinner pan.

8 ounces spaghetti

1 teaspoon salt

¼ cup (½ stick) butter

½ cup onion, minced

¼ cup green bell pepper, minced

1 cup coarsely chopped fresh mushrooms

½ cup heavy cream

2 (12-ounce) cans water-packed tuna, drained

1 cup grated Parmesan cheese

½ cup minced fresh parsley

½ cup grated Parmesan cheese

Bring 2 quarts of water to a boil in a large pot; add the spaghetti and salt. Cook until the spaghetti is al dente.

Melt the butter in a large skillet; add the onion and bell pepper and sauté until tender. Add the mushrooms and cook for 3 to 5 minutes, stirring frequently. Add the cream, tuna, 1 cup Parmesan and the parsley. Divide among the TV dinner trays. Sprinkle with equal portions of ½ cup Parmesan.

YIELD | 8 to 10 TV dinner servings

Gingered Peas and Carrots

1 cup baby-cut carrots, cut into ¼-inch
   pieces
1 (16-ounce) package frozen green peas
⅓ cup orange juice
1 tablespoon sugar
1 teaspoon cornstarch
¼ teaspoon salt
¼ teaspoon ground ginger
1 tablespoon butter or margarine
1 tablespoon minced fresh chives

Cook the carrots in boiling water in a saucepan until tender; drain. Cook the peas according to the package directions; drain.

Combine the orange juice, sugar, cornstarch, salt and ginger in a small saucepan and stir until well blended. Bring to a boil and cook until the mixture thickens slightly, stirring occasionally.

Combine the peas and carrots in a bowl; stir in the orange juice mixture, butter and chives. Place in the second section of each TV dinner tray.

YIELD | 8 to 10 TV dinner servings

Cherry Crisp

Using canned cherry pie filling makes this dessert a breeze.

½ cup rolled oats
½ cup all-purpose flour
¾ cup brown sugar
¾ teaspoon ground cinnamon
¾ teaspoon ground nutmeg
¼ cup chopped pecans
5⅓ tablespoons butter, melted
1 (21-ounce) can cherry pie filling

GARNISH
Sliced almonds

Preheat the oven to 375 degrees.

Combine the oats, flour, brown sugar, cinnamon, nutmeg and pecans in a medium bowl and mix well. Pour the butter over the mixture and mix well.

Place about 2 to 3 tablespoons of the pie filling in the third section of the TV dinner tray. Top with 1 to 2 tablespoons of the oat mixture.

Cover the TV dinners with foil and bake for 20 minutes. Uncover the Cherry Crisp and cook for 10 minutes longer. Garnish with almonds.

YIELD | 8 to 10 TV dinner servings

Have a Ball!

Leaves are changing; there's crispness in the air. This is the perfect time to host an outdoor party. Put on an event that brings out your guests' competitive spirits! Choose a few fun, fast-moving outdoor games that don't require a lot of space. For our "Have a Ball" event we set up stations for chipping, horseshoes, bocce, and beach ball toss.

INVITATION

Write your invitations on beach balls to let guests know it's going to be a playful party. Use a black permanent marker to write the invitations. Deflate the ball, put it in an envelope, and mail it. Guests will have to blow up the ball to read the invitation. (Or, for a fun twist, you can actually blow up the ball, address it, and mail it through the post office. The post office will deliver a ball!) Be sure to write on the ball that guests should bring the ball with them to the party.

ACTIVITY

Set up chipping, horseshoes, bocce, and beach ball toss stations around the yard. Each couple is a team. Give each team a scorecard.

Chipping

You don't have to be a golfer to enjoy a chipping competition. You will need a club called a pitching wedge and six golf balls. Set up a starting area and a chipping area. Set up a chipping area by painting a circle with white spray paint at a good chipping distance from the starting area. Your yard will dictate how far away to locate the circle. (Don't worry about the white paint—it fades quickly, and is gone after mowing.) Players receive 3 balls each. Give participants a few practice shots before they chip each ball. One point is received for each ball that lands in the chipping area (inside the white circle.) Keep track on the teams' scorecards.

Horseshoes

This outdoor game is played between two people (or two teams of two people each) using four horseshoes and two throwing targets (stakes) set in the ground forty feet apart (or whatever distance works with your yard). The object is to ring the stake or throw the horseshoes as close to the stake as possible. Each person throws two horseshoes, alternating sides.

Scoring:
- 1 point if a horseshoe is within one horseshoe's distance from the stake
- 1 point for a leaner—horseshoe rests against the stake
- 2 points for the team with two horseshoes closer to the stake than their opponent's
- 3 points for a ringer—horseshoe completely encircles the stake

Scores are written on the scorecard. Play as many rounds as you wish.

★ MENU ★

SERVE WITH | Sweet potato fries and
Wild Rice and Kidney Bean Salad (page 105)

Bocce

Bocce is normally played on a bocce court but is easy to play in your yard. It is a simple game played with wooden balls. Each team of two gets four balls. Teams choose between red and green balls. Regulation Bocce balls are 4.2 inches (107 mm) in diameter and weigh 2 pounds. There is also a smaller ball called a "jack" or "pallino." A person from each team throws the "jack" wherever they want it in the yard. Then each player takes a turn throwing a bocce ball with the object of landing the ball closest to the jack. (Have a tape measure on hand.) Points go to the team with the ball closest to the jack. Play typically continues to 12 points but you can vary it to fit your party. We normally play to 6 or 8 points so that the game can be played more quickly. Scores are noted on the scorecard at the end of the game.

Beach Ball Toss

As a finale, have your guests get their beach balls. Find an area where each couple can toss their ball up in the air and keep it up in the air by alternating hits between partners. Once the ball falls to the ground or someone hits it twice in a row, that couple is eliminated. Play continues until one couple remains. Score according to how many couples are participating. For example, if there are 10 couples the winning couple gets 10 points, the couple in second place receives 9 points, and so on. Add the couples' scores to the scorecard.

Tally the scorecards and award a prize to the winning couple. You could also have a prize for the lowest score.

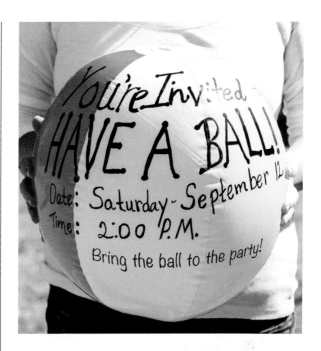

Bourbon Slush

A great drink to keep in your freezer.

8 tea bags

2 cups boiling water

1 to 1½ cups sugar, or to taste

12 ounces orange juice

12 ounces frozen lemonade concentrate

3 cups good quality bourbon

7 to 9 cups cold water

Lemon-lime soda or ginger ale

Steep the tea bags in the boiling water for several minutes; discard the bags. Dissolve the sugar in the hot tea. Combine the tea, orange juice, lemonade, bourbon and the cold water in a large plastic container with a lid. Stir, cover and place in the freezer. Stir the mixture 3 or 4 times a day until frozen to a slush. The slush mixture will be ready in 2 to 3 days.

Fill a Tom Collins glass half to three-fourths full with "slush." Top with lemon-lime soda or ginger ale.

YIELD | 20 drinks

• • •

Piñata Dip

1 pint sour cream

1½ teaspoons seasoned salt

½ teaspoon chili powder

1 cup diced ripe avocado

1 cup diced peeled tomatoes

½ cup crumbled crisp-cooked bacon

2 tablespoons minced green onions

Lemon juice to taste

Salt and pepper to taste

Dash of hot red pepper sauce

Tortilla chips or corn chips

Combine the sour cream, seasoned salt and chili powder in a bowl and mix well. Fold in the avocado, tomatoes, bacon and green onions. Add lemon juice, salt and pepper. Stir in pepper sauce.

Can make 2 hours before serving, omitting avocado, and chill. Add avocado just before serving.

Serve with tortilla chips or corn chips.

YIELD | about 4½ cups

• • •

Lamb Burgers
with Cucumber Sauce

If you have never had a lamb burger, you need to try these!

BURGERS

1 head of garlic, unpeeled

Olive oil

2 pounds ground lamb

¾ cup crumbled feta cheese

1 teaspoon dried oregano

1 tablespoon chopped fresh parsley

¾ teaspoon salt

¾ teaspoon black pepper

4 to 6 pita rounds, toasted and split,
    or 4 to 6 King's Hawaiian buns, toasted

Cucumber Sauce (recipe follows)

1 large fresh tomato, sliced

1 medium red onion, sliced

Preheat the oven to 400 degrees. Cut the top off the garlic to expose the cloves. Drizzle with a little olive oil. Wrap tightly in aluminum foil. Bake for 30 minutes or until tender; cool. Squeeze out the garlic.

For the Lamb Burgers, combine the ground lamb, roasted garlic, cheese, oregano, parsley, salt and pepper in a bowl. Mix gently with your hands. Shape into 4 to 6 patties. Refrigerate.

Preheat the grill to medium-high. Grill the burgers until cooked through. Place on toasted pita rounds or buns. Serve with Cucumber Sauce and slices of tomato and onion.

YIELD | 4 to 6 burgers

CUCUMBER SAUCE

1 seedless cucumber, peeled, grated and dried on paper towels

¾ cup plain Greek yogurt

1 tablespoon minced fresh mint leaves

1 teaspoon red wine vinegar

1 garlic clove, minced

Juice of ¼ to ½ fresh lime

Salt and pepper to taste

Combine the cucumber, yogurt, mint, vinegar, garlic, lime juice, salt and pepper in a small bowl and mix well. Refrigerate until ready to serve.

Yield: about 1 cup

Wilson Burgers

My grandchildren always ask for these burgers when they come for dinner and insisted that this recipe go into the cookbook. I think the horseradish is the "secret" ingredient.

2 pounds ground round

¼ cup finely chopped onion

1 tablespoon Worcestershire sauce

¼ cup ketchup

1 tablespoon horseradish

1 tablespoon yellow mustard

1 teaspoon seasoned salt

½ teaspoon freshly ground pepper

Buns

Cheese, sliced tomato, sliced onion, lettuce leaves and pickles

Combine the hamburger, onion, Worcestershire sauce, ketchup, horseradish, mustard, salt and pepper in a large bowl. Mix gently with your hands, taking care not to overmix. Shape into 4 to 6 patties.

Grill to desired doneness. Serve on buns and with desired toppings, such as cheese, tomato, onion, lettuce and pickles.

YIELD | 4 to 6 burgers

Oriental Slaw

A nice change from traditional coleslaw.

½ head cabbage, shredded

4 green onions, chopped

1 (3-ounce) package beef- or chicken-flavored ramen noodles

½ cup vegetable oil

3 tablespoons balsamic vinegar

3 tablespoons sugar

Seasoning packet from ramen noodles

⅛ teaspoon salt

⅛ teaspoon pepper

GARNISH

½ cup slivered almonds, toasted

3 tablespoons sesame seeds, toasted

Combine the cabbage and green onions in a serving bowl. Break the ramen noodles into small pieces and add to the bowl.

Combine the oil, vinegar, sugar, ramen noodles seasoning, salt and pepper in a jar and shake to mix, or whisk in a bowl. Add to the cabbage mixture and toss to coat. Cover and chill until serving time. Add the almonds and sesame seeds just before serving.

YIELD | 8 servings

TIPS

LEFTOVER WINE | Don't throw out leftover wine. Freeze it in ice cube trays for future use in sauces and casseroles.

Hash Brown Casserole

A classic recipe that is great for a crowd!

1 (16-ounce) package frozen hash brown potatoes

16 ounces sour cream

1 (10-ounce) can cream of chicken soup

½ cup (1 stick) butter, melted

16 ounces sharp Cheddar cheese, shredded

1 medium onion, chopped

Preheat the oven to 350 degrees.

Combine the potatoes, sour cream, soup, butter, cheese and onion in a large bowl and mix well. Spoon into a 9 × 13-inch baking dish. Bake for 1 hour.

YIELD | 8 to 10 servings

• • •

Ice Cream Sandwiches

Guests love ice cream sandwiches, and so do hosts because they can made in advance.

1 (16-ounce) roll chocolate chip cookie dough

1 quart favorite ice cream, or 1 pint each of two flavors of ice cream, slightly softened

Slice and bake the cookies according to the package directions; cool.

Spoon ice cream onto one of the cookies. Top with another cookie. Wrap ice cream sandwiches individually in plastic wrap. Freeze until firm.

YIELD | 10 to 12 sandwiches

Afternoon Tea

When was the last time you held a tea party? Perhaps when you were little and playing with your dolls and miniature tea service. I certainly remember those days; I even convinced my younger brother to join the party by promising him freshly baked chocolate chip cookies. Bring back those days of your youth by hosting a tea party.

In England, where teatime originated, the traditional teatime is usually between four and five o'clock. Afternoon tea actually originated with the French, who serve tea around four in the afternoon. In the United States, most tearooms serve tea between three and five o'clock. Choose the time that best fits your schedule.

★ MENU ★

INVITATION

Tuck invitations into beautiful cloth napkins, or write them on white doilies, and mail to guests. You can find countless templates online to create a tea party invitation.

DECORATIONS

Many of us have silver trays passed down to us through our families. This is the time to bring them out, polish them, and enjoy them. Have a tiered cake stand? It is perfect for a tea party. Have a teapot and teacups? They don't have to match. Have fun shopping in consignment stores for pieces that will make your tea party extra special. Bring out your tablecloths and cloth napkins as well. Set your table using the protocol described below. Fresh flowers would also add to the tea party décor. Give your guests a gift of tea cookies wrapped in netting and tied with a bow as they leave the party.

ACTIVITY AND PROTOCOL FOR AFTERNOON TEA

Set up a table with small clay pots, potting soil, and a variety of herbs. Before the party, paint black chalkboard paint across the front of each pot. After the tea party your guests will go to the table, choose an herb, and plant it in a pot. Have chalk for them to write the name of the herb that they planted. They take the potted herb home as a gift.

Below is the protocol for an authentic English tea. I have included it for fun and for information. Don't let it intimidate you—have fun with it. Use what you want and set the tone you want for your tea party.

Tea

The teapot is placed in front of the hostess, and she pours the first cup of tea for her guests. The idea of "pinkie up" came from early cups that did not have handles. Tea should not be stirred; instead, the spoon should be put into the tea at the six o'clock position and the liquid softly folded toward the twelve o'clock position two or three times. Tea is not used to wash down food; it is to be sipped before eating. Cream is never served with tea, as it is too heavy. Milk is always used and is added after the tea is in the cup. A lemon slice can float in the teacup to enhance the flavor of the tea. Use sugar cubes and sugar tongs in your sugar bowl.

Food

If you use a tiered stand, scones should be placed on the top tier, tea sandwiches on the middle tier, and sweets on the bottom tier. There is a strict protocol for eating a scone. Although in America we see large scones cut into halves and spread with jam and cream, scones should be smaller and eaten by breaking off bite-size pieces. Jam and cream are then applied with a bread-and-butter knife to each individual bite.

Afternoon tea was created to foster friendship, so have fun with it.

(Afternoon tea information is from "Tea Etiquette Faux Pas and other Misconceptions about Afternoon Tea" by Ellen Easton)

Tea

Using filtered or spring water is best for making tea.

1 rounded teaspoon of loose tea, or 1 tea bag

1 cup boiling filtered or spring water

Milk to taste

Sugar cubes to taste

Pour heated tap water into the teapot; swirl it around to heat the teapot. Pour out the water. Add 1 rounded teaspoon of loose tea in a tea ball or 1 teabag per cup of tea. Pour boiling water into the teapot. Let the tea steep for 3 to 5 minutes. Serve with milk and sugar cubes.

YIELD | 1 cup of tea

• • •

Apricot Walnut Tea Sandwiches

A tasty tea sandwich.

1 (10-ounce) jar apricot preserves

8 ounces cream cheese, softened

½ cup chopped walnuts

1 loaf thinly sliced raisin bread, crusts removed

GARNISH

Fresh mint leaves

Combine the preserves, cream cheese and walnuts in a bowl and mix. For each sandwich, spread the preserves mixture over 1 slice of bread and top with another bread slice. Cut to the desired shape and size. Garnish each sandwich with a mint leaf.

YIELD | 20 to 24 servings

Egg Salad Triangles

These are nice as open-faced sandwiches.

8 eggs, hard-boiled, chopped

½ cup mayonnaise

1 teaspoon prepared mustard

½ teaspoon white vinegar

⅛ teaspoon dill weed

Salt and pepper to taste

Thinly sliced pumpernickel bread, crusts removed

GARNISH

Snipped fresh chives

Combine the eggs, mayonnaise, mustard, vinegar and dill weed in a medium bowl and mix well. Add salt and pepper. Cut the bread slices into triangles. Spread with egg salad. Garnish with chives.

YIELD | 10 to 16 triangles

Ham and Cheese Cornucopias

These make a pretty presentation on your tea table.

24 thin ham slices
1 to 2 tablespoons honey mustard
24 thin Swiss cheese slices
½ cup Boursin cheese

Cut the ham and cheese into 4 × 5-inch slices. Spread each ham slice with a thin layer of honey mustard; top with a slice of Swiss cheese. Spread with Boursin cheese. Cut into halves diagonally, forming triangles. Roll into cornucopias and secure with a decorative toothpick.

YIELD | 48 cornucopias

· · ·

Apricot Scones

A delicious tea favorite.

½ cup (4 ounces) dried apricots, chopped
½ cup orange juice
2 tablespoons honey
4 (2-inch) strips orange peel
3 cups all-purpose flour
1 tablespoon baking powder
¼ teaspoon salt
1 cup (2 sticks) unsalted butter, softened
¼ cup sugar
3 large eggs
1 teaspoon vanilla extract
⅓ cup buttermilk

ICING (OPTIONAL)
2 tablespoons orange juice
1½ teaspoons grated orange peel
1 cup confectioners' sugar

Combine the dried apricots, orange juice, honey and orange peel in a small saucepan. Cover and simmer for 10 to 12 minutes or until the apricots are very soft. Discard the orange peel. Mash the apricots to a thick purée.

Mix the flour, baking powder and salt in a medium bowl. Beat the butter with an electric mixer in a large bowl until creamy. Add the sugar and beat for 2 to 3 minutes or until fluffy. Add the eggs, 1 at a time, mixing well after each addition. Beat in the vanilla. Add the flour mixture and mix until blended. Add the buttermilk and mix until blended. Fold in the apricot purée.

Drop by ¼- to ½-cup scoopfuls 2 inches apart onto an ungreased baking sheet. Cover and refrigerate for 1 hour.

Preheat the oven to 350 degrees. Uncover the scones and bake for 15 to 20 minutes or until golden brown.

For the icing, combine the orange juice, orange peel and confectioners' sugar in a small bowl and mix until the sugar is dissolved. Brush over the warm scones.

YIELD | 12 to 14 scones

Raspberry Scones

Another scrumptious scone recipe.

3 cups all-purpose flour

⅓ cup sugar

2 teaspoons baking powder

½ teaspoon baking soda

½ teaspoon salt

14 tablespoons cold unsalted butter, diced (do not allow to soften)

1 cup buttermilk

1 tablespoon lemon zest

¼ cup seedless raspberry jam

2 tablespoons unsalted butter, melted

Preheat the oven to 425 degrees.

Combine the flour, sugar, baking powder, baking soda and salt in a large bowl. Cut in the cold butter with a pastry blender or fork until the mixture resembles coarse meal. Add the buttermilk, 1 tablespoon at a time, and the lemon zest, stirring with a fork to mix.

Gather the dough into a ball and turn out onto a floured surface. Roll into a flat 7- to 8-inch circle. Spread the jam over half of the dough; fold the dough over the jam to cover. Roll the dough into a 12-inch circle. Cut with a sharp knife into 12 to 16 wedges or squares.

Arrange the scones 1 to 2 inches apart on an ungreased baking sheet. Brush the tops with the melted butter. Bake for 12 to 15 minutes or until golden brown.

YIELD | 12 to 16 scones

Cucumber Sandwiches

A traditional tea party sandwich.

1 large seedless English cucumber, thinly sliced

8 ounces cream cheese, softened

¼ cup mayonnaise

½ teaspoon dill weed

¼ teaspoon garlic salt

1 loaf thinly sliced white bread, crusts removed

GARNISH

Finely chopped fresh parsley

Place the cucumber slices between two layers of paper towels and place in a colander for 10 minutes to drain. Combine the cream cheese, mayonnaise, dill weed and garlic salt in a small bowl and mix well. Cut the bread slices into the desired shape and size. For each sandwich, spread cream cheese mixture over 1 piece of bread, top with cucumber slices, overlapping slightly. Top with another bread slice. They may also be served open faced, if desired. Garnish with parsley.

YIELD | 12 to 20 servings

Miniature Party Cakes

Tiny frosted cakes for your tea table. These should be made 1 day ahead of serving so the frosting can set.

CAKES

1 (18-ounce) package yellow cake mix

1 tablespoon grated lemon zest

APRICOT GLAZE

1½ cups apricot preserves

⅓ cup water

3 tablespoons sugar

Fondant Frosting (recipe follows)

Preheat the oven to 350 degrees. Grease a 10 × 15-inch jelly roll pan. Line the bottom and sides with waxed paper or parchment paper; grease the paper.

For the Cakes, prepare the cake mix according to the package directions, adding the lemon zest to the mixture. Pour the batter into the prepared pan. Bake for 25 minutes or until the center springs back when lightly pressed with a finger. Cool on a wire rack for 10 minutes; remove from the pan and cool completely.

Cut the cake lengthwise into 6 strips (do not separate the strips.) Cut the cake diagonally to make 48 diamond-shaped pieces.

For the Apricot Glaze, combine the preserves, water and sugar in a medium saucepan. Cook over medium heat until bubbly. Cook for 3 to 5 minutes longer, stirring occasionally. Pour through a fine sieve.

FONDANT FROSTING

8 cups confectioners' sugar

½ cup water

½ cup light corn syrup

1 teaspoon rum extract or brandy extract

Red and green food coloring, or colors of your choice

Combine the confectioners' sugar, water and corn syrup in the top of a double boiler set over barely simmering water. (Don't let the water boil.) Heat until the frosting is fluid and pourable, stirring frequently. Remove from the heat; stir in rum or brandy extract.

Spear each cake with a fork; dip it in the glaze and place right side up on a wire rack placed over waxed paper to catch drips. Let stand until the glaze is set. (Cakes can be frozen at this point.)

Pour Fondant Frosting over each cake, letting the excess drip down onto the waxed paper. (Drippings can be scraped into a double boiler and reheated and reused.) Let the frosting set until dry and firm.

Divide the remaining frosting between 2 bowls. Add red food coloring to one bowl and green food coloring to the other bowl. Tint the cakes, as desired, with the red and green frosting.

Place the cakes on a tray and cover loosely with waxed paper. Store in a cool place.

YIELD | 48 cakes

Russian Tea Cakes

Make extras and tie them in net bags for your guests to take home. Tea cakes will keep several weeks in a tightly covered container.

2 cups (4 sticks) butter or margarine

1 cup confectioners' sugar

2 teaspoons vanilla extract

½ teaspoon salt

4½ cups all-purpose flour

1 cup ground walnuts

1 cup confectioners' sugar

Preheat the oven to 400 degrees.

Beat the butter and 1 cup confectioners' sugar with an electric mixer in a large bowl until fluffy and light. Beat in the vanilla and salt. Gradually blend in the flour and walnuts to make a stiff dough.

Roll pieces of the dough into 1-inch balls between your palms. Place the balls 1 inch apart on lightly greased cookie sheets. Bake for 12 minutes or until lightly browned.

Remove the hot cookies carefully from the cookie sheets. Roll the cookies in 1 cup confectioners' sugar. Cool completely on wire racks; roll again in confectioners sugar to make a generous white coating.

YIELD | 100 cookies

TIPS

HEADACHE CURE | Have a headache? Take a lime, cut it in half, and rub it on your forehead. The throbbing should go away.

Lemon Tea Muffins

The batter can be baked in loaf pans, if you prefer.

MUFFINS

½ cup (1 stick) butter or margarine, softened

1½ cups sugar

4 eggs

2 tablespoons grated lemon zest

1 tablespoon lemon extract

4 teaspoons baking powder

1 teaspoon salt

1½ cups light cream

2 cups all-purpose flour

1 cup almonds, toasted and chopped

LEMON GLAZE

⅓ cup confectioners' sugar

¼ cup lemon juice

Preheat the oven to 350 degrees. Lightly grease 48 miniature muffin cups.

For the Muffins, cream the butter and sugar with an electric mixer in a large bowl until light and fluffy. Add the eggs, 1 at a time, and beat on high speed for a total of 3 to 5 minutes. Beat in the lemon zest, lemon extract, baking powder and salt. Add the cream and flour alternately and mix gently. Stir in the almonds.

Fill the muffin cups three-fourths full with batter. Bake for 20 to 25 minutes or until lightly browned.

For the Lemon Glaze, combine the confectioners' sugar and lemon juice in a small bowl. Spoon the glaze over the hot muffins. Cool before removing from pans.

YIELD | 48 muffins

Note

To bake as loaves, divide the batter between 2 greased 5 × 9-inch loaf pans and bake for 50 to 55 minutes.

Swamp Soirée

Instead of a traditional Halloween party in October, why not throw a Swamp Soirée? Forget the ubiquitous orange and black, and have a "swamp" setting: fish nets, fishing rods, crab traps, inflatable alligator, and, for extra fun, a fog machine. Go online and download swamp sounds to welcome your guests as they arrive. Make your food "creepy" by placing plastic cockroaches, spiders, and snakes on the food platters. Play a game of Silent Charades to add to the Swamp Soirée theme.

INVITATION

Use clip art on your computer to print an invitation with alligators or other swamp creatures, or put your invitation in a small brown box filled with Spanish moss and a small plastic alligator or snake.

DECORATIONS

Set the scene at the door by hanging Spanish moss around your entryway. Stumps, old fishing poles, crab traps, plastic crabs, and alligators also create atmosphere. Continue the theme inside your home. Use fishing net as a tablecloth. Plastic snakes, flies, and alligators can be scattered around your table and your rooms. Hang Spanish moss or gauze from your chandeliers and lights. Dim your lights and have a fog machine going in the room. (Fog machines can be rented or ordered online, and they are not very expensive.) Cajun music playing in the background completes the swamp theme.

ACTIVITY

In Silent Charades, the charades are all acted out at the same time, and the object is for contestants to guess which other person is acting out their same charade.

Make up two identical cards of each charade phrase. If you have sixteen guests you will need two sets of eight charade cards. Everyone draws a card out of a bowl, studies it, and puts the card in a pocket or someplace safe. As soon as they draw a card there is no talking! On the word "Go!" everyone starts acting out the word or phrase on his/her card. At the same time, contestants should scan the room to determine who else is acting out the same word or phrase. When they think they have found that someone, they go to that person (still no talking!) and they both sit down. When everyone has sat down next to a partner, go around the room to find out if they identified the correct person. You can give a prize to the partners who found their partner first.

Some ideas for charade cards: Ragin' Cajun, Crocodile Dundee, Alligator Alley, swamp buggy, Venus flytrap, grassland airboat, rainforest, water moccasin. Let your imagination run wild to come up with charade cards that set the mood of your party.

★ MENU ★

SERVE WITH | Crusty Bread

Gluhwein

A recipe we brought back from Germany. We always have it ready for our adult "trick-or-treaters" on Halloween night. It is also perfect for a Swamp Soirée!

2 (750-ml) bottles red wine
1 cup sugar
1 cinnamon stick
3 or 4 lemon slices, studded with
  3 or 4 whole cloves each
1 orange, sliced

Combine the wine, sugar, cinnamon stick, lemon and orange in a saucepan. Bring to a boil. Reduce heat and simmer for 20 minutes. Pour into mugs and serve.

YIELD | 12 (4-ounce) servings

. . .

Voodoo Mai Tai

This recipe was given to us by a bartender in Hawaii in the 1970s. He wrote it on a backscratcher for us, and we have had that backscratcher all these years.

½ ounce orange curaçao
½ ounce orgeat syrup
1 ounce white rum
½ ounce dark rum
½ ounce 151-proof rum
2 ounces sweet-and-sour mix
1½ ounces pineapple juice

GARNISH
Pineapple slice

Combine the curaçao, orgeat syrup, white rum, dark rum, 151-proof rum, sweet-and-sour mix and pineapple juice in a cocktail shaker filled with ice. Shake vigorously until the shaker is frosty; strain into a glass filled with ice. Garnish with a pineapple slice.

YIELD | 1 drink

Shrimp Beignets

These are always a favorite!

2 eggs
½ cup milk
8 ounces uncooked shrimp
1 tablespoon Cajun spice
¼ cup finely chopped green bell pepper
½ cup finely chopped green onions
¼ cup finely chopped celery
1 tablespoon finely chopped garlic
½ cup corn kernels
1½ cups all-purpose flour
1 teaspoon salt
1 teaspoon baking powder
Vegetable oil for deep frying
Salt to taste
Rémoulade or Tartar Sauce (page 114)

Beat the eggs in a medium bowl. Add the milk, shrimp, Cajun spice, peppers, green onions, celery, garlic and corn and mix well. Add the flour, 1 teaspoon salt and baking powder and mix gently.

Heat enough oil to cover the beignets in a deep pan to 350 degrees. Drop the batter by tablespoonfuls into the hot oil, taking care not to crowd the pan. Fry for 7 to 10 minutes or until lightly browned. Drain on paper towels and season with salt to taste. Serve with rémoulade or Tartar Sauce.

YIELD | 24 beignets

Crawfish Dip

One of my favorite dips!

¼ cup chopped green bell pepper

½ cup chopped onion

¼ cup chopped green onions

¼ cup (½ stick) butter

1 (10-ounce) can cream of mushroom soup

1 (10-ounce) can Rotel tomatoes with green chilies

1 (16-ounce) package Velveeta cheese, cut into chunks

1 (16-ounce) package frozen fully cooked crawfish

Scoop-shaped corn chips or tortilla scoops

Sauté the bell pepper, onion and green onions in the butter in a medium saucepan. Add the soup, tomatoes and cheese. Cook until the cheese is melted. Add the crawfish. Cook until heated through. Serve with corn chip scoops or tortilla scoops.

YIELD | 8 servings

• • •

Seafood Jambalaya

A full meal in one pot!

2 tablespoons vegetable oil

1½ pounds fresh medium shrimp, peeled and deveined

1 cup chopped onion

½ cup chopped green bell pepper

1 carrot, peeled and chopped

½ cup chopped celery

3 garlic cloves, minced

1 (8-ounce) can tomato sauce

1 (16-ounce) can whole tomatoes, undrained and chopped

2 cups chicken broth

1 cup water

1 cup uncooked long-grain rice

1 teaspoon salt

½ teaspoon dried thyme

½ teaspoon dried basil

½ teaspoon red pepper flakes

½ teaspoon chili powder

½ teaspoon sugar

½ cup chopped fresh parsley

Dash of hot red pepper sauce (optional)

Heat the oil in a Dutch oven over medium heat. Add the shrimp and cook for 4 to 5 minutes or until the shrimp turn pink. Remove the shrimp.

Sauté the onion, green pepper, carrot, celery and garlic in the hot oil for 3 minutes. Stir in the tomato sauce, tomatoes, broth, water, rice, salt, thyme, basil, red pepper flakes, chili powder and sugar. Bring to a boil. Cover, reduce the heat and simmer for 40 to 45 minutes or until the rice is tender and most of the liquid is absorbed, stirring frequently. Stir in the parsley and shrimp and cook for 10 minutes longer. Add the pepper sauce, if desired.

YIELD | 6 to 8 servings

Frozen Grasshopper Pie

A delicious dessert you can prepare ahead of time.

1½ cups finely crushed Oreo cookies
   (about 15 cookies)

Butter

1 cup heavy whipping cream

1 (14-ounce) can sweetened condensed
   milk

3 tablespoons green crème de menthe

2 tablespoons white crème de cacao

GARNISH

Whipped cream, chocolate shavings and
   stem-on maraschino cherries

Reserve 1 tablespoon of the cookie crumbs. Pat the remaining crumbs over the bottom and up the side of a buttered 9-inch pie plate.

Whip the cream with an electric mixer in a medium bowl until peaks form. Fold in the condensed milk, green crème de menthe and white crème de cacao. Spoon into the prepared crust. Sprinkle with the reserved crumbs. Freeze for 4 to 6 hours. (Pie will not be hard when frozen.)

Garnish each serving with a dollop of whipped cream, chocolate shavings and a cherry.

YIELD | 6 to 8 servings

 TIPS

WHIP TIP | To whip cream more quickly, place the bowl and beaters in the freezer for 1 hour before using.

Bring on the Glitz

One of my fondest memories is of my parents hosting their Gourmet Club at our home. My parents had a group of about six couples that gathered bimonthly for a gourmet meal. The hostess always went out of her way to find an exquisite menu because she knew it was her time to shine and prove her culinary skills. My mom would spend days planning her menu and prepping her meal. The night of the dinner, guests would get dressed up in tuxedos and formal gowns. It was quite a sight! My siblings and I would sit upstairs and peer down through the banisters of our staircase in awe at the pomp and circumstance. Of course times have changed since the 1960s, and elegant dinners have taken on a different look. No more tuxedos and formals, but it is still nice to put out a little extra effort sometimes and present an elegant meal for a special occasion. What is wonderful about the following menu is that it is elegant, delicious, and sure to receive lots of "wows!" And best of all, much of it can be prepared ahead of time.

INVITATION

Buy some glitzy card stock and print your invitations on it. You may also find many invitations on various online sites. If you don't mind hand-delivering your invitations, buy plastic champagne glasses, fill them with gold or silver tinsel or confetti, and tuck the invitation inside.

DECORATIONS

Use what you have on hand to make a special table. This is the time to bring out your good china, silver, and crystal. Candles always add a special glow to a table. Splurge on fresh flowers for the table. Type up menu cards for each place setting. Finish your place settings with a bundle of chocolates wrapped in netting and tied with a bow for guests to take home.

For a special touch, freeze a bottle of champagne in a block of ice with flowers. It is very easy to do. On the morning of your party, cut off the top quarter of a half-gallon milk carton. Put the unopened bottle of champagne in the milk carton and fill the carton almost to the top with distilled water. Place flowers (I use roses) on either side of the bottle. Place in the freezer. Right before your guests arrive, peel off the milk carton to expose the beautiful ice block filled with flowers.

SETTING THE TONE

Greet your guests by presenting each woman with a long-stemmed rose. Hand each guest a glass of champagne with Grand Marnier and a strawberry. These touches let guests know they are in for a very special evening. Put together a playlist of your favorite dinner music to play in the background.

★ MENU ★

SERVE WITH | Judy's Yeast Rolls (page 31)

Shrimp Cocktail Ice Bowl

This is sure to get "wows" from your guests, and it is so easy to make! What is fun about this is that each ice bowl is a little different. They don't need to be "perfect"; as a matter of fact, I think that's the charm of these ice bowls—they aren't perfect. These can be made ahead and stored in your freezer until ready to use.

ICE BOWL

1 (8-inch) balloon per guest

Water

SHRIMP COCKTAIL

Shredded lettuce

4 large shrimp with tails intact

Shredded lettuce

Cocktail sauce

To make the ice bowl, fill the balloon with water by fitting the neck of the balloon over the faucet, turning on the water and filling the balloon to the size bowl you want. Tie the balloon and place in the freezer. (Placing the balloons on the shelves of the door of the freezer is easier than placing them in the freezer, but either way will work.) Check the balloons after about 4 hours. You want a thin layer of ice—about ½ inch thick, around the balloon. Test the thickness by gently touching the balloon to feel for the thickness of the ice. If it does not feel thick enough, return to the freezer for an additional 30 minutes. Continue to check every 30 minutes until desired thickness. Do not let the ice get too thick.

Hold the balloon over the sink to catch any water and remove the balloon. Puncture the ice wall and cut as large a hole as you want for your ice bowl. Wrap the ice bowl with plastic wrap and freeze until ready to use.

Place lettuce on a salad plate to hold the water as the ice bowl begins to melt. Place a little shredded lettuce in each ice bowl. Arrange the shrimp in the ice bowl and add 1 tablespoon of cocktail sauce. Serve immediately.

YIELD | 1 serving

Beef Tenderloin
with Caper Mustard Sauce

Always a favorite! The caper mustard sauce is a favorite recipe from my sister.

1 (5- to 7-pound) beef tenderloin, trimmed, at room temperature

1 cup olive oil

Salt

1 garlic clove, finely chopped

¼ cup coarse black pepper

Caper Mustard Sauce (recipe follows)

Preheat the oven to 500 degrees.

Brush the tenderloin with the olive oil and sprinkle with salt. Combine the garlic and black pepper in a small bowl. Press the mixture onto the tenderloin. Place the tenderloin in a baking pan large enough not to crowd it.

Roast for 15 minutes. Reduce the temperature to 225 degrees. Bake for 1 hour and 45 minutes to 2 hours for medium-rare. Remove from the oven; cover with foil. Let stand for 15 minutes before carving. Serve with Caper Mustard Sauce.

YIELD | 8 to 10 servings

Note
Ask the butcher to trim the tenderloin for you.

CAPER MUSTARD SAUCE

3 rounded tablespoons Dijon mustard

2 egg yolks, at room temperature

1 small green onion, chopped

Pinch of marjoram

Juice of ½ lemon (about 2 tablespoons)

1 cup light olive oil

½ cup half-and-half

1½ tablespoons capers, rinsed and drained

Combine the Dijon mustard, egg yolks, green onion, marjoram and lemon juice in a blender or food processor; process until creamy. Add the olive oil in a slow steady stream, processing constantly. Add the half-and-half and capers. Refrigerate until ready to use. May be made a day ahead. Serve at room temperature alongside the tenderloin.

Yield: about 2 cups

TIPS

POTATO SAVER | To keep potatoes from sprouting, place an apple in the bag with the potatoes.

Roasted New Potatoes
with Fresh Rosemary

5 pounds new potatoes

¼ cup olive oil

5 or 6 sprigs fresh rosemary

Salt and pepper to taste

Preheat the oven to 400 degrees.

Cut the potatoes into quarters and place in a large baking dish. Toss with the olive oil and fresh rosemary. Season with salt and pepper to taste. Bake for 30 to 40 minutes or until the potatoes are tender and browned, tossing occasionally.

YIELD | 8 to 10 servings

• • •

Roasted Asparagus

This easy, delicious method can be used on almost any vegetable.

1½ pounds asparagus

Olive oil

Garlic pepper

Preheat the oven to 400 degrees.

Snap any tough ends from the asparagus. Arrange the asparagus in a single layer on a rimmed baking sheet. Coat with olive oil and sprinkle with garlic pepper. Roast for 7 to 15 minutes, depending on the size of the asparagus, watching carefully so asparagus does not burn.

YIELD | 8 servings

Cranberry and Goat Cheese Salad

A favorite recipe from an Army friend. It is my go-to salad for dinner parties.

¼ cup dried cranberries

½ cup tawny Port wine

5 ounces bacon, chopped

2 shallots, minced

1 garlic clove, minced

⅓ cup olive oil

¼ cup red wine vinegar

2 teaspoons sugar

16 ounces mixed salad greens

½ cup pine nuts, toasted

1 small package goat cheese,
    cut into ½-inch slices.

Combine the cranberries and wine in a small saucepan. Bring to a simmer over medium heat. Remove from the heat; let stand for 15 minutes or until the cranberries reconstitute. Fry the bacon in a skillet until crisp. Drain all but 1 to 2 tablespoons of the bacon drippings from the skillet. Add the shallots and garlic and cook for 2 minutes. Add the bacon, olive oil, vinegar and sugar. Cook until the sugar is dissolved, stirring constantly. Stir in the cranberry mixture. (Dressing can be made a day ahead and reheated in the microwave just before serving.)

Toss the salad greens, pine nuts and dressing in a bowl. Divide the salad among salad plates. Top each salad with a slice of the goat cheese.

YIELD | 8 servings

Flaming Baked Alaska

Wow your guests with an impressive finale to your gourmet meal.

- 1 (15-ounce) package brownie mix
- 1 quart French vanilla ice cream
- 1 quart peppermint ice cream
- 5 egg whites, at room temperature
- Dash of cream of tartar
- ¾ cup sugar
- 1 tablespoon crème de cacao
- Half of an empty egg shell, cleaned and dried
- 2 sugar cubes
- Lemon extract

Prepare and bake the brownie in a 9-inch round cake pan according to the package directions. Let cool.

Line a 2½-quart glass or metal bowl (about 9 inches in diameter) with plastic wrap.

Soften the ice cream slightly. Layer ½ inch of the French vanilla ice cream in the prepared bowl. Freeze until firm. Fill the remainder of the bowl with the peppermint ice cream. Smooth the top of the ice cream. Cover with foil and freeze until firm. (The recipe can be prepared ahead of time to this point. Store the brownie layer in an airtight container.)

Beat the eggs whites with an electric beater in a large bowl until frothy. Add the cream of tartar and beat until soft peaks form. Add the sugar, 1 tablespoon at a time, beating well after each addition. Beat until the mixture is satiny and holds soft peaks Beat in the crème de cacao.

Remove brownie from the pan and place on an ovenproof platter. Remove the foil from the ice cream and invert the ice cream onto the brownie. Remove the plastic wrap. Working quickly, spread the meringue over the ice cream, swirling it into peaks. Push the egg shell, open side up, into the middle of the meringue. The top of the eggshell should be even with the top of the meringue. (The recipe may be frozen at this point for up to 24 hours.)

Preheat the oven to 500 degrees. Bake the Alaska in the lower third of the oven for 3 minutes or until lightly browned.

Soak the sugar cubes in lemon extract and place in the egg shell. Ignite with a match. Present the flaming dessert at the table.

YIELD | 12 servings

Note

Many other combinations of ice cream would be equally delicious.

FLAMING BAKED ALASKA

Friends for Dinner

November is the beginning of the busy holiday season; first Thanksgiving and then the busy month of December with Christmas, Hanukkah, and Kwanza. What a great time to take a breath and enjoy an easy evening with friends. This evening is meant to be stress free; no fancy, creative invitations or decorations. Pick up the phone and invite your friends over for a leisurely dinner and drinks. The menu serves 6 to 8 people. Set your table casually. The majority of this meal may be prepared ahead of time so that you have time to enjoy your guests.

★ MENU ★

Kathy's Cosmopolitan

These go down very smoothly, so beware!

2 ounces vodka

1 ounce triple sec

1 ounce Rose's lime juice

1 ounce cranberry juice

GARNISH

1 lime twist

Fill a cocktail shaker with ice; add the vodka, triple sec, lime juice and cranberry juice. Shake until the shaker is frosty. Strain into chilled martini glasses. Garnish with a lime twist.

YIELD | 1 drink

• • •

Cranberry Gin and Tonic

November is the perfect time of year for this drink.

1- to 2-inch strip of orange peel

1 tablespoon fresh or frozen cranberries

1 teaspoon sugar

3 tablespoons gin

1 tablespoon fresh orange juice

¼ cup tonic water

Fill a cocktail shaker with ice; add the orange peel, cranberries, sugar, gin and orange juice. Shake until the shaker is frosty. Pour into an 8-ounce glass. Top off with the tonic water.

YIELD | 1 drink

Ceviche

This is a popular Mexican recipe that has caught on in the United States. Serve in martini glasses for a pretty presentation.

1 pound mahi-mahi or bay scallops

Juice of 6 large limes

1 teaspoon sugar

2 teaspoons salt

Pinch of dried oregano

1 teaspoon white pepper

4 dashes hot red pepper sauce

2 tablespoons finely chopped onion

2 tomatoes, diced

½ red bell pepper, minced

2 tablespoons finely chopped cilantro

GARNISH

Avocado slices

Lime slices

Dice the mahi-mahi. Combine the lime juice, sugar, salt, oregano, white pepper, pepper sauce and onion in a large bowl and mix well. Add the mahi-mahi, immersing completely. (Add more lime juice if needed to cover the fish.) Chill for at least 6 hours.

Drain half of the liquid from the bowl. Add the tomatoes, bell pepper and cilantro and stir gently. Chill thoroughly before serving. Garnish servings with an avocado slice and a lime slice.

YIELD | 4 to 6 servings

CEVICHE

Spinach Cranberry Salad

A recipe from Bob's Enlisted Aide.

CROUTONS

2 cups pumpernickel or rye bread cubes

1 to 2 tablespoons olive oil

SHALLOT DRESSING

2 tablespoons balsamic vinegar

2 tablespoons white wine vinegar

2 teaspoons Dijon mustard

1 shallot, minced

½ teaspoon salt

½ teaspoon pepper

⅔ cup olive oil

SALAD

3 (10-ounce) packages mixed spinach and arugula

1 medium red onion, thinly sliced

1 cup roasted pecans

1 cup dried cranberries

½ cup grated Parmesan cheese

For the Croutons, preheat the oven to 400 degrees. Toss the bread cubes with the olive oil in a bowl. Spread over a baking sheet and bake for 10 minutes, turning twice.

For the Shallot Dressing, whisk the balsamic vinegar, wine vinegar, Dijon mustard, shallot and salt and pepper in a bowl. Add the olive oil in a stream, whisking until emulsified.

For the salad, combine mixed spinach and arugula, onion, pecans, dried cranberries and Parmesan in a large salad bowl. Toss with the Shallot Dressing and top with the croutons.

YIELD | 6 to 8 servings

Mushroom Rounds

Can be made ahead, refrigerated and baked just before serving.

Butter, softened

1½ loaves party rye bread

3 (4-ounce) cans mushroom pieces, chopped

6 slices bacon, cooked and crumbled

1 cup grated Swiss cheese

6 tablespoons mayonnaise

5 tablespoons dried parsley

1 tablespoon lemon juice

Preheat the oven to 400 degrees. Butter the bread slices lightly on one side. Arrange butter side down on a baking sheet. Combine the mushrooms, bacon, cheese, mayonnaise, parsley and lemon juice in a medium bowl and mix well. Spoon some of the mushroom mixture onto each piece of bread. Bake for 5 to 7 minutes or until the cheese is melted. Serve hot.

YIELD | 20 rounds

• • •

Marinated and Grilled Flank Steak

This recipe from my parents has a different flavor than most flank steak recipes.

1 (1½-pound) flank steak

1 cup dry vermouth

½ cup soy sauce

4 large or 6 small garlic cloves, minced

3 tablespoons minced fresh parsley

Score both sides of the flank steak diagonally in both directions in a diamond pattern. Combine the vermouth, soy sauce, garlic and parsley in a large resealable plastic bag; shake to mix. Add the flank steak, seal and marinate in the refrigerator for at least 3 hours or up to a day ahead.

Remove the meat from the marinade and grill to desired degree of doneness. Let the steak stand for a few minutes before slicing thinly on the diagonal. Marinade can be heated and served with the steak, if desired.

YIELD | 6 to 8 servings

• • •

Double-Baked Potatoes

A make-ahead side dish that's always welcome.

6 to 8 baking potatoes

¼ cup (½ stick) butter

½ cup (about) milk

1 to 2 cups shredded Cheddar cheese

2 green onions, chopped

Salt and pepper to taste

Paprika

Pierce the potatoes using a knife to allow steam to escape. Microwave the potatoes until tender, or bake in a 400-degree oven for 30 to 40 minutes or until a fork pierces the potatoes easily. Cut off the top fourth of the potatoes and scoop out the pulp, leaving a ¼-inch shell.

Combine the potato pulp and butter in a medium bowl. Whip with an electric mixer to blend. Beat in the milk gradually to desired consistency. Add the Cheddar cheese, green onions, salt and pepper and stir gently to mix. Fill the potato shells with the

mixture, mounding slightly. Sprinkle with paprika. Arrange the potatoes in a shallow baking dish and refrigerate until ready to bake.

Preheat the oven to 375 degrees. Bake the potatoes for 20 to 25 minutes or until heated through.

YIELD | 6 to 8 servings

• • •

Roasted Brussels Sprouts

1½ pounds Brussels sprouts, cleaned and cut into halves

Olive oil

Salt and pepper to taste

4 slices pancetta, chopped

¼ cup chopped walnuts

Preheat the oven to 425 degrees.

Arrange the Brussels sprouts on a rimmed baking sheet. Coat with olive oil. Season with salt and pepper to taste. Sprinkle the pancetta evenly over the sprouts. Bake for 10 to 12 minutes or until the brussel sprouts are nicely browned. Sprinkle with the walnuts and bake for 3 to 5 minutes longer, watching closely so the walnuts do not burn.

YIELD | 6 to 8 servings

 REMOVE SPLINTERS | When you get a splinter, try Scotch tape before using tweezers or a needle. It will take it out easily and painlessly.

Adobe Pie
with Kahlúa Chocolate Sauce

A delicious dessert from a Texan Army friend. The Kahlúa Chocolate Sauce is delicious on so many desserts! You can substitute any two ice cream flavors that sound good to you. Be sure to make the Kahlúa Chocolate Sauce 24 hours in advance.

PIE

1 cup chocolate cookie crumbs

¼ cup sugar

¼ cup (½ stick) unsalted butter, melted

1 pint premium butter pecan ice cream, softened

3 tablespoons Kahlúa Chocolate Sauce (recipe follows)

1 pint premium coffee ice cream, softened

3 tablespoons Kahlúa Chocolate Sauce

TOPPING

1 cup heavy whipping cream

3 tablespoons Kahlúa

2⅔ cups Kahlúa Chocolate Sauce

Stir the cookie crumbs, sugar and butter in a medium bowl until moist and crumbly. Pat evenly over the bottom and up the side of a 9-inch pie pan. Freeze for 1 hour.

Spread the butter pecan ice cream over the crust, filling half the pie pan. Spread 3 tablespoons of the Kahlúa Chocolate Sauce over the ice cream. Freeze until the ice cream is firm. Spread with the coffee ice cream, mounding it slightly in the middle. Spread 3 tablespoons of the Kahlúa Chocolate Sauce over the coffee ice cream, using a knife to swirl the sauce over the top of the pie. Freeze until firm. Wrap well with plastic wrap. (Pie can be kept in freezer for up to 1 week.)

For the Topping, whip the cream until soft peaks form. Fold in the Kahlúa. Warm the Kahlúa Chocolate Sauce. Spoon some sauce over each serving of the pie and top with a dollop of the whipped cream.

YIELD | 6 to 8 servings

Note

Chocolate cookies and chocolate cookie crumbs are sometimes hard to find, so I buy Oreo cookies, remove the cream in the middle and crumble the chocolate cookies.

TIPS

LONGER-LIVED CANDLES | Candles will last longer if placed in the freezer for about 3 hours prior to burning.

KAHLÚA CHOCOLATE SAUCE

¾ cup (1½ sticks) unsalted butter

6 ounces semisweet chocolate, chopped

¾ cup plus 2 tablespoons sugar

¾ cup lightly packed cocoa powder

1½ teaspoons instant espresso, or sifted instant coffee powder

½ cup corn syrup

¾ cup heavy whipping cream

½ cup Kahlúa

1 teaspoon vanilla extract

Melt the butter and chocolate together in a medium saucepan over low heat until smooth, stirring occasionally. Whisk in the sugar. Sift in the cocoa powder, whisking to blend. Add the espresso and corn syrup. Whisk in the cream and Kahlúa. Bring to a boil, stirring frequently. Reduce the heat and simmer for 5 minutes, stirring once or twice and scraping down the side with a rubber spatula. Remove the sauce from the heat and stir in the vanilla.

Pour the sauce into a container with a lid. Cool completely, cover and store in the refrigerator for at least 24 hours to mellow the flavor and texture. To serve warm, heat in the microwave just until warm.

Yield: about 3 cups

Café Toledo

A perfect ending to a relaxing evening. Try topping with the leftover whipped cream from the Adobe Pie.

1 part amaretto

1 part Kahlúa

1 part Bailey's Irish Cream

3 parts brewed coffee

Whipped cream

Measure the amaretto, Kahlúa and Irish Cream into a coffee cup. Fill with hot coffee. Top with whipped cream.

YIELD | 1 cup

Holiday Party

December is such a festive time of the year. Family and friends probably get together more often this month than any other. We want it to be a month filled with joy and fellowship. We try to avoid the stress that can creep in when we are trying to do so much for so many. Let's plan a fun, fuss-free holiday party and gift exchange.

INVITATION

Since this is the season for baking, why not bake gingerbread men (page 185) and attach your invitations to them? It's a tasty invitation that previews the treat your guests will get at your upcoming Holiday Party. Another idea is to attach invitations to candy canes. If you are having a gift exchange, be sure to explain it clearly in your invitation.

ACTIVITY

A gift exchange is almost a given at holiday parties, because who doesn't like to get a gift? There are many different ways to do them: ornament exchanges, wine exchanges, and "white elephant" exchanges. Or you can simply set a price point and let guests decide what kind of gift to bring. You decide what type of gift exchange sounds good.

Try a fun, new twist to a gift exchange and call it "Holiday Trivia." Guests draw a number (16 guests; numbers 1 to 16). The person with #1 selects a gift and opens it. The next person must answer a holiday trivia question before choosing a gift. If they answer correctly, they have the option of taking the first person's gift or selecting one from the gift pile. If not, they can only select from the gift pile. (We allowed couples to help each other with answering the question.) Continue until all your guests have a gift. The #1 person gets another turn, but must answer a trivia question this time. If they answer it correctly, they can choose to take a gift from anyone or they may keep the gift they have.

★ MENU ★

IDEAS FOR HOLIDAY TRIVIA

Sample Questions

1. How many points/sides does a snowflake have?
2. The movie Miracle on 34th Street is set in what city?
3. Who is rumored to have stolen Christmas?
4. How many reindeer hooves are there, including Rudolph?
5. What were Frosty's last words?
6. If you were born on Christmas day what is your horoscope sign?
7. Joseph, Mary, and Jesus left Bethlehem for what country?
8. Lucy charges how much for her psychiatric services in A Charlie Brown Christmas?
9. What is the biggest selling Christmas single of all time?
10. Frosty was brought to life by what?
11. Name 3 reindeer whose names start with "D."
12. What was the last state to declare Christmas as a legal holiday in 1907?
    a) California
    b) Massachusetts
    c) Oklahoma
    d) Indiana
13. In what country does the poinsettia originate?
14. Who made the song "White Christmas" famous?
15. On the twelfth day of Christmas what did "my true love bring to me"?
16. What does Santa do to go back up the chimney after delivering the toys?

Answers

1. 6
2. NYC
3. Grinch
4. 36
5. "I'll be back again someday."
6. Capricorn
7. Egypt
8. 5 cents
9. White Christmas
10. Magic hat
11. Dasher, Donner, Dancer
12. Oklahoma
13. Mexico
14. Bing Crosby
15. 12 Drummers Drumming
16. Places his finger next to his nose

Cranberry Kisses

A festive holiday drink.

2 cups cranberry juice cocktail

1 cup vodka

½ cup amaretto

3 tablespoons fresh orange juice

Ice cubes

GARNISH

6 Clementine segments

Mix the cranberry juice, vodka, amaretto and orange juice in a pitcher. Cover and chill until ready to use. Can be made 1 day ahead and refrigerated.

Fill a cocktail shaker with ice cubes. Add 1 cup of the vodka mixture. Cover and shake vigorously. Strain into 2 martini glasses. Garnish with Clementine segments. Repeat for the remaining drinks.

YIELD | 6 drinks

• • •

Hot Spiced Rum

A great drink for a cold night.

1 cup heavy whipping cream

2 tablespoons maple syrup

¼ cup dark rum

⅓ cup hot water

2 tablespoons ginger liqueur

Freshly grated nutmeg

Beat the cream and maple syrup with an electric mixer in a bowl for 2 minutes or until the mixture is the consistency of softened butter. Cover and chill for 1 to 24 hours.

Combine the rum, hot water and ginger liqueur in a 6-ounce cup. Top with ¼ cup of the maple cream mixture and sprinkle with nutmeg.

YIELD | 6 drinks

• • •

Vegetable Crudités
with Italian Dip

For a very festive presentation, serve on a tray with the vegetables arranged in the shape of a Christmas Tree.

CRUDITÉS

1 bunch fresh broccoli, broken into florets

1 head cauliflower, broken into florets

Pint of cherry tomatoes

Baby-cut carrots

ITALIAN DIP

16 ounces sour cream

1 envelope Good Seasons Italian salad dressing mix

For the Crudités, arrange the broccoli, cauliflower, tomatoes and carrots on a serving platter.

For the Italian Dip, mix the sour cream and salad dressing mix in a small bowl. Chill for at least 1 hour or up to 24 hours. Serve with the crudités.

YIELD | 10 to 12 servings

Note

For an interesting presentation, cut off the top of a bell pepper and remove the membranes and seeds. Spoon the dip into the bell pepper for serving.

PINE CONE CHEESE BALL

Pine Cone Cheese Ball

Pretty on your buffet table.

- 1¼ cups whole natural almonds
- 8 ounces cream cheese, softened
- ½ cup mayonnaise
- 5 bacon slices, crisp-cooked and crumbled
- 1 tablespoon chopped green onion
- ½ teaspoon dill weed
- ⅛ teaspoon pepper

GARNISH

- Artificial pine sprigs or fresh rosemary sprigs
- Crackers

Preheat the oven to 300 degrees.

Spread the almonds in a single layer in a shallow pan. Bake for 15 minutes or until the almonds begin to change color, stirring every 2 to 3 minutes. Let cool.

Combine the cream cheese and mayonnaise in a bowl and mix well. Stir in the bacon, green onion, dill weed and pepper. Cover and chill for at least 8 hours.

Shape the mixture into 2 small pine cone shapes or 1 large pine cone shape and place on a serving platter. Beginning at the narrow end, press almonds into the cheese mixture at a slight angle in overlapping rows. Garnish with artificial pine sprigs or fresh rosemary sprigs. Serve with crackers.

YIELD | 10 to 12 servings

Grilled Garlic Pepper Salmon Fillet

So simple and so delicious! Be prepared: it won't last long on your buffet table!

- 1 fresh salmon fillet, skin on one side
- 1 to 2 tablespoons olive oil
- Garlic pepper
- Toasted baguette slices or water crackers

GARNISH

- Honey mustard, whipped cream cheese and capers

Place the salmon fillet on a rimmed baking sheet. Brush both sides with the olive oil. Sprinkle with garlic pepper, covering the fillet completely.

Heat a grill to medium-high. Place the salmon skin side down on the grill. Grill for 20 to 25 minutes or until the salmon is nearly cooked through. Turn gently and grill for 10 minutes longer.

Remove the skin and the brown flesh from the fillet. Serve the whole fillet on a platter with toasted baguette slices or water crackers and garnish with honey mustard, cream cheese and capers.

YIELD | 10 to 12 servings

 TIPS

PREVENT STAINS | Spray plastic storage containers with nonstick cooking spray before pouring in tomato-based sauces—no more stains!

Beef Tenderloin
with Horseradish Sauce

Great served hot or cold.

1 (5-pound) beef tenderloin

1 liter Dr. Pepper (not diet)

½ cup soy sauce

Juice of 3 lemons

1 tablespoon peppercorns

1 tablespoon coarse salt

3 garlic cloves, crushed

Horseradish Sauce (recipe follows)

Rolls

Combine the tenderloin, half the Dr. Pepper, soy sauce, lemon juice, peppercorns, salt and garlic in a large resealable plastic bag; add additional Dr. Pepper to cover. Seal the bag. Marinate in the refrigerator for at least 5 hours or up to 24 hours, turning occasionally.

Heat a grill to medium-high. Remove the tenderloin from the marinade and grill until the meat reaches 135 degrees on a meat thermometer for medium-rare, turning to brown all sides. Let stand for 15 minutes before slicing. Serve with Horseradish Sauce and rolls.

YIELD | 15 to 20 servings

• • •

Stuffed New Potatoes

The potatoes may be cooked and scooped in advance.

12 (1½- to 2-inch) new potatoes

2 tablespoons butter, melted

1 teaspoon Dijon mustard

HORSERADISH SAUCE

8 ounces sour cream

2 tablespoons prepared horseradish

2 tablespoons lemon juice

1 tablespoon Worcestershire sauce

½ teaspoon pepper

Dash of hot red pepper sauce

Garnish: Snipped fresh chives

Mix the sour cream, horseradish, lemon juice, Worcestershire sauce, pepper and pepper sauce in a small bowl. Garnish with chives.

Yield: 1¼ cups

¾ cup shredded pepper jack cheese

8 bacon slices, crisp-cooked and crumbled

Salt to taste

GARNISH

Sour cream

Chopped green onions

Preheat the oven to 425 degrees.

Cut the potatoes into halves. Scoop out potato pulp using a melon scoop, leaving a ¼-inch shell.

Whisk the butter and Dijon mustard in a medium bowl. Add the potato halves and stir to coat. Arrange the potatoes cut side down on a greased baking sheet. Sprinkle with salt. Bake for 20 to 30 minutes.

Mix the cheese and bacon in a small bowl. Turn the potatoes right side up; fill the potatoes with the cheese mixture. (The potatoes may be prepared to this point and held at room temperature for 2 hours.) Bake for 5 minutes or until heated through. Garnish with sour cream and green onions.

YIELD | 6 servings

Lemon Bars

These are also excellent slightly frozen.

2 cups all-purpose flour

½ cup confectioners' sugar

½ cup shortening

½ cup (1 stick) butter, softened

4 eggs

1¾ cups sugar

⅓ cup fresh lemon juice

¼ cup all-purpose flour

½ teaspoon baking powder

Confectioners' sugar to taste

Preheat the oven to 350 degrees.

Sift the flour and confectioners' sugar into a large bowl. Combine the shortening and butter in a bowl and beat with an electric mixer until blended. Cut the butter mixture into the flour mixture until the mixture clings together. Press into the bottom of a 9 × 13-inch baking pan. Bake for 20 to 23 minutes or until light golden brown.

Beat the eggs with an electric mixer in a bowl. Add the sugar and lemon juice and mix well. Stir in the flour and baking powder. Pour over the baked crust. Bake at 350 degrees for 25 minutes. Refrigerate for at least 2 hours. Sprinkle with confectioners' sugar to taste and cut into squares right before serving.

YIELD | 50 squares

Note

To freeze, cool the baked bars, cover with foil and freeze. Thaw slightly, dust with confectioners' sugar and cut just before serving.

Gingerbread Cookies

A fun baking project for parents and children.

2 cups all-purpose flour

1 teaspoon baking powder

½ teaspoon baking soda

1 teaspoon ground ginger

1 teaspoon ground cloves

1½ teaspoons ground cinnamon

½ teaspoon ground nutmeg

½ teaspoon salt

½ cup shortening

½ cup sugar

½ cup molasses

1 egg yolk

Currants

GARNISH

Cinnamon drops or ornamental frosting

Combine the flour, baking powder, baking soda, ginger, cloves, cinnamon, nutmeg and salt in a medium bowl.

Beat the shortening with an electric mixer in a large bowl until creamy; stir in the sugar and molasses. Add the egg yolk and mix well. Stir in the flour mixture.

Preheat the oven to 350 degrees.

Roll the dough about ¼ inch thick on a lightly floured surface. Cut with a gingerbread man cookie cutter. Arrange on ungreased baking sheets. Add currants for eyes. Bake for 10 minutes; cool. Garnish as desired.

YIELD | 8 to 15 cookies

Crème de Menthe Brownies

Not only delicious but also attractive on the holiday table.

BROWNIES

1 cup sugar

½ cup (1 stick) butter, softened

4 eggs

1 teaspoon vanilla extract

1 cup all-purpose flour

½ teaspoon salt

1 (16-ounce) can Hershey's chocolate sauce

FILLING

½ cup (1 stick) butter, softened

2 cups confectioners' sugar

2 tablespoons crème de menthe

CHOCOLATE FROSTING

1 cup chocolate chips

6 tablespoons butter

Preheat the oven to 350 degrees.

For the Brownies, combine the sugar, butter, eggs, vanilla, flour, salt and chocolate sauce in a large bowl and mix well. Spread in a greased 9 × 13-inch baking pan. Bake for 25 to 30 minutes; cool and refrigerate.

For the Filling, beat the butter and confectioners' sugar with an electric mixture until creamy. Beat in the crème de menthe. Spread over the cooled brownie layer and refrigerate until cold.

For the Frosting, melt the chocolate chips and butter in a small saucepan, stirring to blend; cool. Spread over the Filling. Refrigerate for at least 1 to 2 hours. Cut into small squares.

YIELD | 12 to 14 servings

Christmas Tree Inspection

When we were at the War College in Carlisle, Pennsylvania, we got a knock on our door one evening. There stood our neighbors, saying they had come to conduct a "Christmas Tree Inspection." We had no idea what they were talking about, but fortunately we invited them in and offered them a drink. It's a good thing we did because they immediately checked off the first item on their check sheet. They then proceeded to our Christmas tree to inspect it, checking off items on the sheet. Fortunately, we passed, and they asked us to join them as they went to other neighbors' homes. Of course, we immediately said, "Yes!" Thus began an annual tradition we took with us from Post to Post. It has always been a hit so I am including it in *At Ease*!

It's a very simple and fun holiday activity that works both on military installations, where it's practical to walk from home to home, and in civilian neighborhoods where friends are spread out. Even friends who don't have Christmas trees for religious or other reasons enjoy being part of this festivity, so be sure to invite them along on your inspections.

To hold your Christmas Tree Inspection party, use the "Christmas Tree Inspection Checklist" (page 189). The "inspection" can be a complete surprise for the participants, like our first inspection, but there's a risk that people will be away or otherwise engaged. Or you can invite participants for dinner at your house, giving a starting time an hour later than the start time for your inspection. That way you know they'll be home and not busy. Knock on the first door, do the inspection, then bring that couple along to the next home and so on until you've inspected all the homes. The group then comes to your house for dinner from a menu that's easy to make ahead and set out when you return.

This gathering has been a big hit wherever we go, and I know you and your friends will enjoy it. Adjust it to fit your neighborhood and the number of people you want to invite. It is very adaptable to a number of variations!

★ MENU ★

DECORATIONS

The wonderful thing about this party is that your home is already decorated with your holiday decorations. Make the entry equally festive by lining the walk to your front door with luminaries. These are simple to make. Fill brown paper sandwich bags with about two inches of sand or cat litter. Place a votive candle inside. Appoint someone to light the candles for you at an appointed time so they're burning when the guests arrive.

MENU

Buffet style is the way to go. Choose a make-ahead menu and put all the food on serving platters. If you have a helper, ask them to set the platters on the serving table, or plan to do it yourself once you and your guests arrive at your home.

ACTIVITY

For the Christmas Tree Inspection, make a copy of the "Christmas Tree Inspection Checklist" for every home you plan to visit (or make up a checklist of your own). The inspected couple is invited to join the inspection team immediately after documenting said inspection results.

To keep the spirit going, a fun notice to add to the inspection is: *"If failing inspection, a no-notice inspection will be conducted within the next 30 days."*

Christmas Tree Inspection Checklist

1. Were we offered Christmas libations immediately after being greeted at the door?
   ☐ YES   ☐ NO

2. Is there a Christmas tree in the house?
   ☐ YES   ☐ NO

3. Are there twinkling lights on the tree?
   ☐ YES   ☐ NO

4. Is there tinsel on the tree?
   ☐ YES   ☐ NO

5. Is there a patriotic decoration conspicuously displayed on the tree?
   ☐ YES   ☐ NO

6. Is there an angel on top of the tree?
   ☐ YES   ☐ NO

7. Are there presents under the tree?
   ☐ YES   ☐ NO

8. Is there a toy train encircling the tree?
   ☐ YES   ☐ NO

9. Is there Christmas music playing in the background?
   ☐ YES   ☐ NO

10. Are there stockings hung by the chimney with care?
    ☐ YES   ☐ NO

11. Is there mistletoe hanging in the doorway?
    ☐ YES   ☐ NO

12. Is there a Texas decoration displayed proudly for all to see?
    ☐ YES   ☐ NO

One point deduction for groveling: _____

Passing score is 75% (9 out of 12 points): _____

Official initials: _____

PROTESTS—NOT AUTHORIZED!

Artillery Punch

Made in 1819 in honor of President Monroe.

3 cups water

½ cup instant tea

Fifth of bourbon

Fifth of claret

2 cups orange juice

1½ cups dark Jamaican rum

1 cup lemon juice

¾ cup dry gin

¾ cup brandy

4 to 6 (10-ounce) packages frozen
    strawberries, thawed

Ice ring

Combine the combine water and tea in a large bowl and stir until the tea is dissolved. Add the bourbon, claret, orange juice, rum, lemon juice, gin and brandy.

Purée the strawberries in batches in a blender; add to the punch. Let stand, covered, for several hours. Serve with an ice ring in a 1-gallon punch bowl.

YIELD | 45 to 60 (4-ounce) servings

TIPS

SALT SOP | If you accidentally oversalt a dish, while it is still cooking, drop in a peeled potato—it will absorb the excess salt.

Marinated Shrimp
in Ice Bowl

The ice bowl is impressive and easy to make!

2½ quarts water

3 pounds uncooked large shrimp, peeled
    and deveined

4 small red onions, thinly sliced

8 bay leaves

1 (3-ounce) jar capers, drained

1 tablespoon sugar

¼ teaspoon salt

1 cup olive oil

½ cup red wine vinegar

½ cup good-quality balsamic vinegar

2 tablespoons fresh lemon juice

1 tablespoon Worcestershire sauce

½ teaspoon hot red pepper sauce

Ice Bowl (page 192)

Bring the water to a boil in a large saucepan. Add the shrimp and cook for 3 to 5 minutes or until the shrimp turn pink. Drain and rinse with cold water.

Layer the shrimp, onions, bay leaves and capers in a large shallow dish. Combine the sugar, salt, olive oil, red wine vinegar, balsamic vinegar, lemon juice, Worcestershire sauce and pepper sauce in a medium bowl and mix well. Pour over the shrimp mixture. Cover and chill for 8 to 24 hours, stirring occasionally. Drain before serving in the Ice Bowl.

YIELD | 8 to 10 servings

MARINATED SHRIMP IN ICE BOWL

ICE BOWL

Distilled water

Fresh flowers, such as a variety of roses and daisies

Fresh fruit slices (optional)

Garnish: Lettuce

Place a 1½-quart bowl inside a 4-quart bowl. Hold the small bowl in the center of the large bowl and add just enough distilled water to the large bowl to make the bowls' rims even. Remove the small bowl. Place some flowers and fruit in the water and freeze. Remove from the freezer. Place the small bowl in the center of the layer of ice in the large bowl. Tape the bowls across the top to keep the small bowl centered. Fill the space between the bowls with distilled water. Arrange flowers and fruit in the water. Return the two bowls to the freezer, keeping the bowls level. Freeze for at least 8 hours.

When ready to use, remove the bowls from the freezer and let stand for a few minutes. Remove the tape. Pour some hot water into the small bowl and twist until it pops out. To remove the ice from the larger bowl, wrap a warm dishtowel around the bowl to loosen it. (A blow dryer also works.) Avoid running very hot water on the bowl, as it might crack.

Place the Ice Bowl on a rimmed tray garnished with pretty lettuce to hold the water as the ice melts.

Baked Rice with Almonds

Can prepare up to the baking step early in the day. Bake 2 hours before serving.

6 tablespoons butter or margarine

2 cups long-grain white rice

⅓ cup slivered almonds

1 (10-ounce) can beef consommé

2 soup cans water

Salt and pepper to taste

Preheat the oven to 275 degrees.

Toast the almonds in the oven (or in a small skillet over low heat) just until golden brown. Increase the oven temperature to 300 degrees.

Melt the butter in a skillet over low heat. Add the rice and cook until lightly browned, stirring occasionally. Stir in the toasted almonds.

Spoon the mixture into a deep baking dish. Add the consommé, water, salt and pepper. Cover and bake for 1½ to 2 hours, stirring frequently. After 1 hour, if the liquid does not seem to be absorbing fast enough, remove the cover to finish baking.

YIELD | 10 servings

Beef Bourguignon

This recipe was given to me by a dear friend back in the 1980s, and I still pull it out for a great make-ahead dinner for parties. This recipe doubles successfully.

4 bacon slices, cut into ½-inch pieces

3 pounds lean boneless beef, cut into 1-inch cubes

Vegetable oil (optional)

2 to 4 cups good dry red wine

1 (15-ounce) can beef bouillon

1 tablespoon tomato paste

1 teaspoon dried thyme

1 teaspoon salt

Freshly ground pepper to taste

1 bay leaf

3 garlic cloves, minced

12 small boiling onions

1 cup fresh mushrooms, quartered

1 to 2 tablespoons butter

3 or 4 carrots, peeled and cut into 1- to 2-inch pieces, or baby carrots

1 tablespoon all-purpose flour

Salt and pepper to taste

Minced parsley

Sauté the bacon in a large heavy skillet until crisp; place in a baking pan. Brown the beef in the bacon drippings, until browned on all sides, adding oil if needed. Transfer the beef to the baking pan.

Preheat the oven to 350 degrees.

Deglaze the skillet with a small amount of wine, scraping up the browned bits. Pour the liquid into the baking pan. Add the beef bouillon, tomato paste, thyme, salt, pepper, bay leaf and garlic. Add enough wine to almost cover the meat. Cover and bake for 1 to 2 hours, basting occasionally and adding additional wine or bouillon if the mixture starts to get dry.

Peel the onions and cut a small cross in the stem end to prevent the onions from coming apart while cooking. Sauté the mushrooms in the butter for 3 to 4 minutes. Add the onions, mushrooms and carrots to the baking pan and mix well. Cover and bake for 1 hour longer.

Drain the pan drippings into a large saucepan. Remove ¼ cup of the pan drippings and mix with the flour in a cup. Gradually add the flour mixture back to the saucepan of pan drippings, stirring constantly. Cook until thickened, stirring constantly. Season with salt and pepper. Pour over the beef and vegetables and bake for 5 minutes or until heated through. Sprinkle with minced parsley.

YIELD | 6 servings

Note

The Beef Bourguignon may be cooked over low heat on the stove for 2 hours.

English Walnut Salad
with Poppy Seed Dressing

The dressing is delicious on almost any salad.

ENGLISH WALNUT SALAD

1 head romaine

1 head Bibb lettuce

½ cup red chopped onion

1 cup English walnuts, chopped

3 oranges, peeled and cut into segments

POPPY SEED DRESSING

1 cup vegetable oil

½ cup sugar

⅓ cup cider vinegar

1 tablespoon poppy seeds

1 tablespoon finely chopped onion

1 teaspoon salt

1 teaspoon dry mustard

For the English Walnut Salad, combine the romaine, Bibb lettuce, onion, walnuts and oranges in a salad bowl and toss to mix.

For the Poppy Seed Dressing, process the oil, sugar, vinegar, poppy seeds, onion, salt and dry mustard in a blender or food processor until thick.

Pour desired amount of the dressing over the salad and toss to coat.

YIELD | 6 to 8 servings

Chocolate Kahlúa Trifle

Use a glass trifle bowl so all the pretty layers are visible. The trifle is also nice layered in individual parfait glasses. Best made a day ahead so the flavors can mingle.

1 (18-ounce) package Swiss Chocolate cake mix

2 (3-ounce) packages instant chocolate pudding mix

3 cups milk

¾ to 1 cup Kahlúa

4 Heath bars, crushed

1 (16-ounce) container whipped topping

1 (2-ounce) package slivered almonds, toasted

Prepare and bake the cake in a 9 × 13-inch baking pan according to the package directions. Cool completely. Cut the cake into bite-size pieces.

Prepare the pudding using 3 cups milk for 2 packages of pudding mix.

Assemble the trifle in layers in the following order: half the cake, ½ cup Kahlúa, half the pudding, one-third of the candy and half the whipped topping. Repeat the layers of cake, Kahlúa, pudding, candy and whipped topping. Sprinkle with the remaining candy and the toasted almonds. Cover and refrigerate.

YIELD | 8 to 10 servings

Irish Coffee

A favorite after-dinner drink.

- 1 cup hot strong black coffee
- 1 heaping teaspoon sugar
- 2 ounces Irish whiskey
- 1 tablespoon cold heavy cream

Warm a stemmed wine glass or an Irish coffee glass by filling with boiling water. Pour out water; pour the coffee into the glass; add the sugar and stir to dissolve. Add the whiskey. Hold a teaspoon, curved side up across the glass and pour the cream over the spoon. Do not stir the cream into the coffee; it should float on top.

YIELD | 1 drink

 TIPS

WAX ON GLASS | To remove wax from a glass-top table, carefully scrape off as much as you can, using a knife or fingernail. Then use a blow dryer to melt the remaining wax. Dab with a paper towel and then clean with glass cleaner.

Index